Active Parenting

ACTIVE
PARENTING

Teaching Cooperation,
Courage, and
Responsibility

MICHAEL POPKIN

PERENNIAL LIBRARY

HARPER & ROW, PUBLISHERS, SAN FRANCISCO
Cambridge, Hagerstown, New York, Philadelphia, Washington
London, Mexico City, São Paulo, Singapore, Sydney

Library of Congress Cataloging-in-Publication Data

Popkin, Michael.
  Active parenting.

  Bibliography: p.
  Includes index.
  1. Parenting.   2. Child rearing.   I. Title.
HQ755.8.P66 1987   649'.1   85-51033

ISBN 0-06-254061-0

87 88 89 90 91 RRD 10 9 8 7 6 5 4 3 2 1

Contents

Preface

Imagine yourself in this situation: You've just accepted a job as co-captain of an ocean liner. You will be expected to be in charge twenty-four hours a day for approximately eighteen to twenty years. For this privilege, you will pay well in excess of $100,000. You will receive no training whatsoever and no operating manual except for a twelve-page pamphlet entitled "Helpful Tips for Ocean Liner Captains." To complicate matters, your only seafaring experiences to date have been a week-long cruise you once took with your parents as a child (you got seasick) and a sailboat ride around an island and back when you were a counselor in a summer camp. Your co-captain has had even less experience.

What I'm describing, of course, is the situation that our society has traditionally deemed appropriate for parents as they begin their heroic task of preparing the next generation of human beings to run the planet. Compared to the importance and difficulty of *this* challenge, captaining an ocean liner is, you might say, child's play.

Carl Sagan, in *The Dragons of Eden*, reminds us of Jacob Bronowski's wonderful observation: "We have made a kind of bargain with nature: Our children will be difficult to raise, but their capacity for new learning will greatly enhance the chances of survival of the human species." Anybody who doesn't believe that human children are difficult to raise has probably never done it. And as for the importance of child rearing, I believe that the future of any society depends first and foremost on the quality of its parenting.

Active Parenting, an organization founded in 1980, is based on two simple beliefs:

1. Parenting well is extremely important.
2. Parenting well is extremely difficult.

And it is based on three additional assumptions:

1. Most parents have sufficient love and commitment to parent well . . .
2. but have not been given sufficient information, skills, and support.
3. This can be disastrous in our modern society where children openly reject traditional parenting methods.

Everywhere, we find parents and children engaging in frustrating struggles for power to the extent that families often become an energy drain and source of disappointment rather than the network of support and the source of satisfaction that they could be. Worse, many children are not developing the basic qualities necessary for thriving in our modern society: courage, responsibility, and cooperativeness. Consequently, many parents of young children fear the choices their children will make when they become teenagers. This fear may be well-founded since during the last decade we have seen teenage drug use, pregnancy and abortion, crime, and suicide all increase significantly.

Obviously, parents are not the only influence on a child's development, but how they parent is the one element we can do the most about. This simple fact has spawned an increasing number of books and programs designed to aid parents as they raise their children. Schools, churches and synagogues, mental health centers, and community groups offer a variety of courses as such organizations expand their commitment to family life.

Where once such pioneering programs as Parent Effectiveness Training (PET) and Systematic Training for Effective Parenting (STEP) stood alone in the field, today numerous alternatives exist from which parent educators can choose. One such program, *Active Parenting: A Video-Based Program*, forms the basis of this book. With this program, produced in 1983, Active Parenting became the first widespread parent education course to make use of a video-based teaching system. Parents in the more than 2,500 Active Parenting groups throughout the world are responding enthusiastically to this multimedia approach.

But even with the growth of Active Parenting, courses are still not available to most parents. In addition, many of the thousands of Active Parenting alumni are still hungry. Particularly, they are requesting more examples of applications of the Active Parenting methods.

This book is a response to both of these needs. If you are new to Active Parenting, this book offers you the complete Active Parenting approach in a format that fits *your* schedule. Perhaps after reading it, you'll want to help organize an Active Parenting video-based group in your community. If you have already completed a program, I think you will find this a helpful supplement to—as well as a timely review of—the material you have already experienced.

Whatever else you may do, if you have children, then you've also accepted the challenge of being a parent. You're underpaid and overworked, of course, but the satisfactions of doing the job well are worth the effort. And the fact that you are a part of a generation of parents that has the courage to learn will make it far easier for you to steer a successful course.

As you leave the safety of the harbor, keep in mind that these are not uncharted waters. Other parents have gone before you. Professional educators, such as I, have studied children's ways and learned much about what works and what doesn't work with them. This book is a synthesis of that information, and with it in hand, you needn't set out to sea without a clear knowledge of what lies ahead. You have the collective experience of many others as your map.

This is not to imply that personal experience is invalid. I cherish the twenty-seven years I spent in summer camp, from the time I was an infant (my father was the camp director) through my years as a camper, counselor, and division leader, until I became director of a camp myself. The kids in those camps taught me a lot, often about the sense of fulfillment that comes with helping a child grow; sometimes about humility and the limits to my power. (I sometimes joke that two or three of the "less cooperative" campers may have driven me into training as a family therapist.) And I value greatly my experiences as a psychologist in a mental health system and as a therapist in private practice. The families who have shared their lives with me have taught me much, just as they have learned much.

But no matter how enriching personal experience may be, its lessons are small in comparison with those we can glean from the collective experience of humanity. This is the essence of education: that we can go beyond our own limited experience and learn from the great reservoir of human experience.

You already know a tremendous amount about children. This book will help you integrate that knowledge into a method of parenting that has proven effective for millions of parents. Equipped with such a set of tools, you will be better able to take full advantage of your own experience.

Bon voyage!

PART I

The Theory of Active Parenting

1

What's Your Style as a Parent?

*All the production of peoples, all
urging forward, the destruction of old
barriers and prejudices, usually happen
for the sake of the progeny and are
meant first of all to help them.*

ALFRED ADLER

Danny Clarke is a five-year-old boy with dark brown hair and, depending on your perspective, either an angelic smile or a devilish grin. He shows a penchant for video games and an aversion (often irate) to picking up his toys. He lives in a city apartment with his divorced mother and two goldfish (Ronnie and Fritz). His mom works and is often pretty well "fried," as she puts it, by the time she picks Danny up from child care.

3

On Tuesday, his mom was in the kitchen preparing dinner and Danny was in the living room protecting the planet from alien invaders. Teeth clenched and thumb pressing the video joystick in megabursts of pulsating energy, he may as well have been in another galaxy. At least he was far enough gone that he totally missed his mother's first two calls to dinner. He didn't miss the third.

His mother was already backhanding the off button on the TV, sending the alien invaders back into the oblivion in which they dwelt, when she looked down at him and commanded, "Didn't you hear me calling? Dinner's getting cold. Now, get in that kitchen right now!"

"No." The word is simple. It is eloquent. It is infuriating.

"What did you say?"

"No. I don't have to!"

"Now you listen to me, Danny. You get in that kitchen right now or you're going to get a spanking!"

"No. I don't have to. You can't make me!"

Danny's mother's hand reared back in perfect form, lifting to the apex of its ancient arch; then, as if a maternal heat-seeking missile, it dived toward its appointed target.

"Smack!" It struck Danny's behind with all the pent-up frustration of a bad day at the office. In fact, the blow was about more than video games, defiance, and dinner getting cold. It was about the tie-up on the expressway that had caused her to be fifteen minutes late to work that morning. It was about Phyllis's having been out sick and her having to pick up the Stockman report, and the color having been wrong on the new brochure. In short, it was about everything that was wrong with her life and the world on this Tuesday.

Danny's eyes flooded with pain and indignation. Genuine hatred, black and ugly, surged in his heart, pulsated once through an open artery and shot into his brain, then out his mouth in the awful words, "I hate you! I hate you!"

As Danny ran to his bedroom to bury his wounds facedown in a pillow, his mother slumped to her knees in disgust. "How did this happen again?"

The Active Parent

Danny and his mother are playing out a scene that happens over and over again in households throughout the world. A child is slow to cooperate—the parent reacts. A child misbehaves—the parent reacts. A child is openly defiant—the parent reacts. It is as if parents are the figures on the video screen, reacting to whatever buttons the child pushes, rather than the thinking, *active* human beings they really are, beings who are able to make their own choices and *act* accordingly.

Many parents wait until their child pushes them to their limit; then they *react*, often with frustration, anger, and random discipline. This is, as one mother put it, "the screech and hit" school—what I call the reactive approach. When parents react rather than act, they allow the child to control the situation, as well as the parent's emotions. Problems tend to continue or even get worse as parent and child *re*-act the same frustrating scene over and over and over. Danny's mother is not the leader in this situation. Leaders make plans of action; they make choices, and then they act. Danny's mother only reacts to whatever he throws up at her.

The philosophy behind Active Parenting is that the parent, rather than the child, should play the leadership role in the family. This book will help you clarify your own goals for your child and teach you effective methods for leading your child toward them. Later in this book, we'll analyze exactly how parents get hooked into the type of reactive exchange that Danny and his mother end up having so often. And, of course, you'll learn a number of techniques—actions—that *you* can use in similar situations. Your *actions* will lead the way.

I chose to emphasize the word *active* in this book for other reasons, also. This is an age of people engaged in a host of active pursuits; jobs and careers, community work, political causes, the arts, hobbies, and sports. By beginning to read this book, you have shown that you are one of these active people; you are taking steps toward improving the interactions in your family, and you are seeking information that will help you to excel as a parent.

Finally, this book is active in another sense: it asks for your involvement in the learning process. I am not interested in having you read this book, tell your friends how wonderful it is, and then do exactly the same things with your child that you have been doing. My goal is for you to first learn to apply some of the methods presented in these pages—maybe it will be just two or three new skills that you pick up; maybe it will be a complete overhaul of your approach to being a parent—and *then* to tell your friends how much you've changed.

To get the most out of this experience, please take the time to complete the activities designated on the Action Pages. Many of these involve doing something with your child that will help sharpen your new skills. Keep in mind that active learning is effective learning. As you'll be admonished in the chapters on discipline, "Don't just sit there; do something!"

I am frequently asked how old a child must be before the methods presented in this book can be used successfully. Over the years, we have heard from parents who report success with toddlers as well as with older teens. In fact, parents often point out that they use many of these skills in all aspects of their lives, even at work or with their friends. The reason for such a wide range of effectiveness is that Active Parenting teaches basic human relationship skills. You will use these techniques differently, however, with a two-year-old than with a ten-year-old or teenager, so I've included examples of children of different ages throughout the book. These examples, your own common sense, and the advice of other parents will help you determine what works best at what age. If you would like to know more about what children are like at different ages, a book on the stages of development might be a useful supplement.*

A Word of Caution About Mistakes

When you read this book, you will learn a very practical model for understanding and leading children. This model, based in part on the work of psychiatrists Alfred Adler and Rudolf Dreikurs and extended by others, has been used effectively by millions of parents, counselors, teachers, and psychologists. It works.

However, it is put into action by human beings, and human beings, as we all know, are imperfect. We make mistakes. As you read this book, you will probably become aware of two kinds of mistakes of your own.

First, you will realize or recall mistakes you have made in the past. Almost everyone does. It is important that you recognize these mistakes, but it is much more important that you *let them go.* They are in the past, and it is useless to dwell on them now. How much better it is to concentrate on being a more effective parent in the present!

Second, you will make new mistakes as you learn these new skills. Mistakes are part of the learning process, and everyone trying new skills makes some. Accept your mistakes without punishing yourself for being imperfect. If you are too hard on yourself, you not only make yourself feel bad, you also put limits on your learning. When we feel criticized, even by ourselves, we become defensive. Soon we don't even admit our mistakes to ourselves, and we lose the valuable opportunity to correct and improve our performance. Mistakes are for learning; please be gentle with yourself.

---

*See the Related Reading section at the end of this book for specific suggestions, and for the titles of works by other psychologists whose names I mention.

ACTION PAGE 1

Accepting our own imperfection is vital to learning. The following affirmation is meant to help you clear the way for excellence as a parent.

Step 1: Read the affirmation through once.

Step 2: If you agree with what it says, read the affirmation through again, slowly. Breathe deeply as you let the words deeper into your belief system.

Step 3: If you are having trouble, write the affirmation line by line on a blank sheet of white paper. Pause after each line, and be aware of any thoughts or feelings that you have.

Step 4: If you are still having trouble forgiving yourself for your imperfections, repeat this affirmation daily until it feels comfortable to you.

THE PARENT'S AFFIRMATION OF IMPERFECTION

It's perfectly okay for me to be imperfect. This includes not being a perfect parent. This means that it's okay that I have already made a lot of mistakes as a parent and that it's okay that I will make other mistakes in the future. What's not okay is for me to pretend that I am perfect and to thereby hide my mistakes from myself. Instead, I will catch my mistakes—with a smile rather than a kick—and learn what they have to teach me. That way, I won't make the same mistakes too often, and I'll become a better and better parent. But I'll never be a perfect parent, and that's okay, because my goal is excellence, not perfection.

Styles of Parenting

Parents are a lot like artists, and parenting and painting have something very important in common. Just as some distinct styles of painting (like classical, impressionist, and modern) have emerged at different points in history, so too have some distinct styles of parenting: autocratic, permissive, and democratic. As with art, these parenting styles are characterized by clear differences of approach and purpose and can be associated with different periods in history (more on this in Chapter 2). Just as the atmosphere of an impressionist museum differs from that of a museum of modern art, so autocratic, permissive, and democratic homes have differing atmospheres. And just as all impressionist painters are similar in style, all democratic parents share certain common principles and techniques.

But let's imagine that you are touring the *Jeu-de-Paume*, the wonderful impressionist museum in Paris. Although all the paintings share certain qualities, you have no trouble (even if you are a novice) distinguishing the soft pastels of a Renoir from the bold and brilliant brushstrokes of a Van Gogh. Each artist has a unique style. Likewise, no two families are exactly alike. You may consciously choose one of the three parenting styles for yourself, but how you interpret and apply that style will be unique to you. For this reason, you needn't worry about accepting everything in this book. You are free to pick and choose what fits your own developing style as a parent, and to leave the rest alone.

This book advocates the democratic style of parenting (in Chapter 2 I'll explain why this style is best suited for the age in which we live), but how you use these techniques may be as different from how the parent next door does as a Renoir is from a Van Gogh. This is a beautiful part of the unique relationship that you are building with each of your children. (I only ask that you don't follow Van Gogh's example and cut off your ear—at least not in front of the children.)

We'll take a closer look at the different parenting styles in a moment, but you might first be interested to learn which style you are currently using. Before reading on in this chapter, take a few minutes to complete the Action Page that begins on page 9.

A Closer Look at Parenting Styles

Now that you have some notion about your own style as a parent, let's take a closer look at these three most common styles. Keep in mind that these styles are not absolute. You may find yourself, at different times, showing characteristics of two or even all three approaches. Many parents swing back and forth between the permissive and autocratic styles, depending upon their frustration level at the time. Without a clear approach to parenting, it's easy to do. One of the goals of this book is to provide you with a clear set of principles and skills so that you become more and more consistent as a parent.

The Autocratic Style

An autocrat desires absolute control, and the autocratic parent is all-powerful where the lives of his or her children are concerned. The parent is a dominating, authoritarian figure who uses reward and punishment as tools to enforce his or her orders. Children are told what to do, how to do it, where to do it, and when to do it. They have very little room to question, challenge, or dissent. Because the autocratic style assumes that people are at worst evil, or at best dangerous, the emphasis in this style is on limiting the child's behavior. Obedience becomes the goal of parenting, and children are believed to learn this lesson best through a mixture of reward and punishment.

Autocratic educators often speak of "breaking the child's will," as if

ACTION PAGE 2

IDENTIFYING YOUR PARENTING STYLE

The following questionnaire is divided into two parts with fifteen statements each. Part I is designed to help you identify your beliefs about being a parent. Part II focuses on your current home situation. As you read each statement, decide how much you agree with it. Then write, in the blank provided or on a separate sheet of paper, the number from 1 to 5 that corresponds to your level of agreement:

■ **1** strongly disagree
■ **2** disagree
■ **3** neutral
■ **4** agree
■ **5** strongly agree

PART I: BELIEFS

_____ **1.** It is better to give a little ground and protect the peace than to stand firm and provoke a fight.

_____ **2.** Children need discipline that hurts a little so that they will remember the lesson later.

_____ **3.** Children shouldn't always get their way, but usually we ought to learn to listen to what they have to say.

_____ **4.** The parent-child relationship is like a war in which if the parent wins, both sides win, but if the parent loses, both sides lose.

_____ **5.** If parents provide a good environment, children will pretty well raise themselves.

_____ **6.** The parent's role is like that of a teacher who is preparing the child for a final exam called life.

_____ **7.** Childhood is so short that parents should do everything to make it a happy time.

_____ **8.** Spare the rod and spoil the child is still the best policy.

_____ **9.** Children need to learn what they may or may not do, but we don't have to use punishment to teach.

_____ **10.** Whether we like it or not, children have the last word about what they will or won't do.

_____ **11.** If you let children have a pretty free reign, they will eventually learn from the consequences of their behavior what is appropriate.

_____ **12.** Children first have to learn that the parent is boss.

_____ **13.** Too many children today talk back to their parents when they should just quietly obey them.

_____ **14.** If we want children to respect us, we must first treat them with respect.

_____ **15.** You can never do too much for your child if it comes from genuine love.

PART II: ACTIONS

_____ **16.** I often have to call my child more than once to get her or him out of bed in the morning.

_____ **17.** I have to constantly stay on top of my child to get things done.

_____ **18.** When my child misbehaves, he or she usually knows what the consequences will be.

_____ **19.** I often get angry and yell at my child.

ACTION PAGE 2 *(continued)*

____ **20.** I often feel that my child is taking advantage of my good nature.

____ **21.** We have discussed chores at our home and everybody takes part.

____ **22.** My child gets a spanking on the average of at least once a month.

____ **23.** My child has no regular chores around the home, but will occasionally pitch in when asked.

____ **24.** I usually give my child clear instructions as to how I want something done.

____ **25.** My child is a finicky eater, so I have to try various combinations to make sure he or she gets the proper nutrition.

____ **26.** I don't call my child names, and I don't expect to be called names by my child.

____ **27.** I usually give my child choices between two appropriate alternatives rather than telling my child what to do.

____ **28.** I have to threaten my child with punishment at least once a week.

____ **29.** I wish my child wouldn't interrupt my conversations so often.

____ **30.** My child usually gets up and ready without my help in the morning.

SCORING YOUR QUESTIONNAIRE

To determine your style as a parent, first transfer your score for each item to the blanks beside the following item numbers listed in parentheses. (Put your score for item #2 in the first blank, item #4 in the second blank, and so on.) Then add your scores in each row across, and put the sum in the blank labeled Total.

Autocratic belief score: **TOTAL**

(2)____ + (4)____ + (8)____ + (12)____ + (13)____ = ____

Permissive belief score:

(1)____ + (5)____ + (7)____ + (11)____ + (15)____ = ____

Democratic belief score:

(3)____ + (6)____ + (9)____ + (10)____ + (14)____ = ____

Autocratic action score:

(17)____ + (19)____ + (22)____ + (24)____ + (28)____ = ____

Permissive action score:

(16)____ + (20)____ + (23)____ + (25)____ + (29)____ = ____

Democratic action score:

(18)____ + (21)____ + (26)____ + (27)____ + (30)____ = ____

To get a clearer look at how your scores on the three styles compare, transfer each of the six totals to the appropriate blank in the table below. To get your combined scores, add your belief score and your action score for each of the three styles. Put these numbers in the blanks in the "Combined" column.

	BELIEF	ACTION	COMBINED
Autocratic	_____ +	_____ =	_____
Permissive	_____ +	_____ =	_____
Democratic	_____ +	_____ =	_____

ACTION PAGE 2 *(continued)*

INTERPRETING YOUR SCORES

The highest combined score possible for each style is 50. The higher your score, the more you tend toward that style of parenting. Your highest combined score, therefore, suggests the style of parenting you are *currently* using. If either of the other combined scores is within fifteen points of your highest score, consider your use of the two styles about equal. The greater the difference among scores, the greater your current preference for the style with the highest score.

Differences of more than fifteen points between belief scores and action scores for any style suggest that you tend to believe one thing, but do another. Do not be alarmed by this. It is common and understandable. As you move through this book, you will probably develop a greater consistency between what you believe and what you do.

HIGH AUTOCRATIC SCORE   If you're like most people, you'll find yourself more autocratic than you thought you were. But after all, this was the predominant style parents used when you were growing up. If you scored highest on this style, you probably find yourself in frequent battles with your child. Anger and frustration probably characterize the power struggles that you and your child experience. You are probably reading this book to find some relief, as well as a more successful approach.

However, a word of caution: many of the ideas presented here will at first appear unreasonable to you. You may especially have trouble with Chapter 2, which presents the democratic model. You may even feel like abandoning the book. That is certainly your choice. But if you can muster the courage to hang in there, you will probably find that these ideas begin making more and more sense to you. More important, you will find that you already possess the strength of will to use the skills that you will be learning as you become an even stronger and more effective parent.

HIGH PERMISSIVE SCORE   In an attempt to avoid being autocratic, you may have overcompensated and developed a permissive style. If you are in this group, your relationship with your child may be pretty good as long as you do what your child wants. But you probably find that your child gets very hostile, and perhaps even throws tantrums, when you do say no or make a demand of him or her. Your relationship is characterized by service and pleasing, but only in one direction. You may have already begun to resent this unfairness. If so, you probably scored higher on the autocratic scale than you expected. It is easy to get fed up with a permissive approach and flip back to an autocratic one.

This book will probably be easy for you to read. You can expect to like the democratic concepts and related techniques. They will probably appeal to your basic stance of respect for your child. But applying the actual discipline will require your time and the courage to be firm. You may feel that it just takes too much time or that you hate to see your child unhappy. Be on guard against reading this book without following through with action.

HIGH DEMOCRATIC SCORE   If you scored highest on the democratic style, your relationship with your child is probably already positive. Though problems certainly occur, an atmosphere of mutual respect, trust, and teamwork enables you to handle them without the hurt or resentment that characterize the other styles.

While autocratic parents may have more difficulty accepting the theory of this book than applying the techniques, and permissive parents may have more difficulty following through than accepting it, your biggest hurdle has already been passed. Because democratic parents have usually already done some reading or even taken a parent education course, they sometimes fall victim to the mistaken belief that they now know it all. The fact that you are reading this book indicates that you are still open to hearing new ideas and learning new skills.

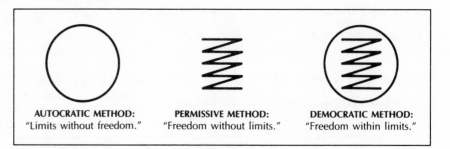

AUTOCRATIC METHOD:
"Limits without freedom."

PERMISSIVE METHOD:
"Freedom without limits."

DEMOCRATIC METHOD:
"Freedom within limits."

something evil in children has to be stamped out before they can take their place in society. Consequently, children have very little freedom in an autocratic system, and very few choices. This style of parenting, characterized by limits without freedom, might be depicted graphically as a closed circle.

The Permissive Style

Permissive parents react strongly against the harsh and uncompromising character of the autocratic method. They assume that people are not only basically good but are capable of self-regulation, and that given sufficient freedom, children will learn through their own direct experience most of what they need to learn. Individual liberty is of paramount importance in this style.

Permissive parents allow their children to "do their own thing." In such households, order and routine are minimal, and few limits to anyone's freedom are imposed. Many such parents behave like rugs, allowing their children to walk all over them. One of the main drawbacks of this style is the insecurity that it produces in children; they grow up having almost no sense of belonging or of cooperation. The permissive method can be described as freedom without limits, and might be signified graphically as a squiggly line, meaning freedom run rampant.

The Democratic Style

The democratic style is, in some respects, a synthesis of the autocratic and permissive styles. In a democratic household, freedom is an ideal, but so are the rights of others and the responsibilities of all. This requires that reasonable limits be placed on individual freedom for the welfare of the group. This concept of freedom within limits is a hallmark of the democratic style, which might be represented as a squiggly line within a circle.

Neither a dictator nor a doormat, the parent in a democratic family is a leader who encourages cooperation and stimulates learning. He or she is also a leader who establishes order and routine, using discipline that respects those who are led. Because every member of a democratic family is an important part of the whole, each feels that "we're in this together"—far different from the "me-against-you" feeling that often exists in autocratic and permissive families.

In Chapter 2, we will explore the democratic style more fully, how it came into being, and more important, why it works better with modern children than the other approaches. Then in Part II, we'll cover the specific techniques of democratic parenting, techniques that have already given millions of parents the means to become the strong and caring leaders that their children need.

What About My Spouse?

While differences in parenting styles between husband and wife are not uncommon, such differences are also not often helpful, and, in fact, can become damaging to the child if the differences become exaggerated. Working with families who have come to me for counseling, I have noticed a frequent, yet disturbing occurrence over the years. Parents who may have slightly different parenting styles when their child is young begin to counterbalance what they see as the negative tendencies of their spouse. One parent, seeing the other as too autocratic, tries to make it up to the child by becoming a little more permissive. The other parent, fearing that the child might become spoiled, becomes more autocratic to make up for the softening tendencies of the permissive spouse. This counterbalancing eventually produces a large gap between the parents, where originally only a small, and relatively harmless, one had existed.

A huge difference in styles—particularly the autocratic-permissive counterbalancing—can be very damaging to a child's ability to learn where the limits in a family really are; since that can retard social growth, it is important for parents to take some steps to keep this from happening. Here are some suggestions:

1. Talk to your spouse about how the two of you will approach your work as parents. If this book makes sense to you, *ask* your spouse to read it to "see what you think." Then use it as a common starting place to decide how the two of you will approach matters.

2. If the two of you agree on a common style, meet regularly to discuss particular situations and discipline options. Keep talking. Encourage each other.

Comparison of Parenting Styles

	AUTOCRATIC	PERMISSIVE	DEMOCRATIC
Goal for self	■ power ■ ease	■ peace ■ ease	■ guidance ■ satisfaction
Accompanying belief	"I must control my child."	"I must please my child."	"I must lead my child."
Parent's goals for child	■ obedience ■ respect for authority ■ a "healthy fear" ■ responsibility to others	■ freedom ■ respect for self ■ a "go for it" mentality ■ responsibility to self	■ cooperativeness ■ respect for self and others ■ courage ■ responsibility to self and others
Discipline tools	■ rewards ■ punishment ■ threats ■ bribes ■ yelling ■ demanding	■ pleasing ■ hoping ■ pleading ■ giving in ■ giving up	■ logical consequences ■ "I" messages ■ natural consequences ■ family meetings ■ negotiation ■ asking
Characteristics of parent-child relationship	■ power struggle ■ anger ■ rebellion ■ coldness ■ distrust	■ service by parent ■ demands by child ■ resentment	■ warmth ■ sharing ■ mutual respect ■ conflict resolution
Qualities of parent	■ controlling ■ critical ■ harsh ■ loud ■ strong	■ indecisive ■ accepting ■ timid ■ inconsistent; when frustrated, parent may swing to autocratic style, then back ■ weak ■ absent	■ firm ■ kind ■ encouraging ■ cooperative ■ strong
Typical qualities of child	■ disobedient ■ sneaky ■ strong-willed ■ rebellious ■ lacking in self-discipline	■ disrespectful ■ spoiled ■ insecure ■ self-centered ■ lacking in self-discipline	■ cooperative ■ responsible ■ courageous ■ team-centered ■ self-disciplined
History	■ dominant until 1950s ■ still used by most parents because it's what they know	■ backlash to autocratic style ■ popular in 1950s and 1960s ■ in busy families, often happens by default	■ has been gaining popularity since 1970s ■ few parents raised this way, but logical commonsense approach makes it easy to teach and learn

3. If your spouse either doesn't want to talk about it or has very strong feelings about a different style from yours, try to win him or her over. See the Appendix for more on this.

4. If you are unsuccessful at winning your spouse over, don't be alarmed. The main purpose of this book is to help you improve *your* relationship with your child. Your child will benefit from that improvement, and your spouse may see a positive effect and begin to change without realizing it.

5. If a difference in styles persists, be on your guard against the natural tendency to counterbalance each other. Also, try to get your spouse to at least agree that the two of you will not sabotage each other by letting your child play one of you against the other. Denied a request by one parent, no child worth his or her salt will miss the opportunity to ask the other parent in hopes of getting a more favorable reply. Agree to consult with each other often. Ask your child if he or she has already asked the other parent, then back your spouse up *even if you think he or she is wrong.* It's okay for you to let your child know that the two of you disagree, but that you refuse to undermine each other.

6. There are exceptions to backing up your spouse. When the risk of real harm exists, *both* parents should agree that they *each* must assent to allowing the child to take the risk. Finally, although it is an unpleasant exception, if you recognize that your spouse is doing something obviously harmful to your child (as in the case of abuse or incest), then you must have the courage to contact someone who can help—either your local community mental health center, Child Protective Services, (a branch of the State Department of Human Resources with offices in most major cities; see your phone book), or, in emergencies, the police.

CASE 2

We've already seen an autocratic parent in action when we witnessed Danny's mother approach his preoccupation with video games at dinner time by using threats, yelling, and punishment, and we've seen the defiance, the hurt feelings, and the retaliation that this approach elicits. Here is how a permissive parent might handle the same situation.

Allison Coleman is an adorable seven-year-old girl. Her mother, a young lawyer with an old firm, often feels guilty about the long hours she must work if she is ever to "make partner." To make it up to Allison, she constantly bends over backward trying to please her. Allison's father, a computer programmer, supports his wife's career and usually gets dinner ready in the evening. Unfortunately, he too is pretty much a "soft touch" when it comes to his daughter.

Allison has one brother, Dexter. At sixteen, Dexter is a good student, a good athlete, and popular. He is convinced that his parents are spoiling Allison rotten, but as long as she stays out of his room, that's their problem.

On the same Tuesday that Danny and his mother were engaged in their power struggle, Mr. Coleman came into the playroom to call Allison to dinner. Dexter was at basketball practice and would eat later. Mrs. Coleman was at work, and would eat even later.

Meanwhile, Allison was building a space station out of plastic blocks. "Allison, honey, are you ready for dinner?" Dad asked pleasantly.

"Not now, Daddy. I'm not finished yet."

"But Allison, dinner's ready, and it won't taste good cold."

"In a minute."

"Okay, Allison, but don't be long."

Ten minutes later:

"Allison? Come on, baby, it's getting cold." No reply from Allison.

"Allison? Do you want me to put it in the oven and keep it warm for you?"

"Yeah," replied Allison without looking up.

An hour later at the table:

"Allison, you're not eating, sweetheart."

"I don't like this chicken."

"But I cooked it last week and you loved it."

"It tastes funny. Daddy, can I have a hot dog?"

"No, baby. This chicken is better for you."

"I hate it! Pleeeeease, can I have a hot dog?"

"Come on, sweety, just try a few bites."

"No! I won't eat."

"Oh, all right. I'll make you a hot dog, but just tonight."

Comment: Mr. Coleman, in his ill-advised attempt to constantly placate Allison, is keeping the peace, but at what price? Allison is not learning how to cooperate and get along with others. Rather, she is becoming self-centered and demanding.

Allison's father is *permitting* her to control the situation as she turns him into a short-order cook. As Danny's mother was controlled by her autocratic style, Mr. Coleman is equally controlled by his permissive style.

CASE 3

The Bradfords live in a beautiful home beside a beautiful lake. Dr. Bradford earns a good salary, and his wife is thinking of expanding her business now that the kids are getting older (Lisa, sixteen; Jason, eleven; Susan, nine). Still, the parenting problems they face are similar to those faced by every family. Mrs. Bradford, having grown tired of ineffectively going back and forth between permissive and autocratic styles of parenting, has finally broken her pattern; her new behavior offers a good example of the democratic style of parenting. Here is her account of dinner at the Bradford house:

"Dinner at our house never seemed to go like it was supposed to. Getting everybody to the table at the same time was the big problem. Actually, getting Jason to the table at the same time as everybody else was the big problem. I guess with two sisters and a mother around all afternoon he probably felt a little like a crown prince. I have to admit, my catering to his whims didn't help. I would coax him to the table or let him eat on a snack table in front of the TV, and get fed up and yell and scream until nobody enjoyed their meal.

"Finally, I realized that I was being controlled, as well as ineffective. So, I came up with a different way to approach the problem. I told Jason that dinner would be served at 6:30 in the dining room and that he was expected, out of common courtesy, to be on time.

"At 6:30, the rest of the family sat down to dinner, but no Jason. The TV was still blaring in the den, so I knew that he was testing me. We began serving, and I waited ten minutes before removing his place setting. (Okay, I'm still a little lenient.) About 6:55, Jason strolled in and asked to be served (the prince had arrived). When I calmly reminded him that I had already explained that dinner would be served at 6:30, he became indignant. He stomped and raged a little, and even beseeched my husband to intervene. Fortunately, I had briefed him about my plan, and he backed me to the hilt.

"I told Jason that breakfast would be served at 7:30 A.M. sharp and that he could try again then. He moped off to his room, but guess what? He was at breakfast the next morning at 7:15 and hasn't missed dinner again since."

Comment: Jason's mother, having experienced the pitfalls of either fighting or giving in, decides to do neither. Instead, she decides what *she* will do, and lets Jason decide what *he* will do. By sidestepping his challenge, she simply goes about her business of serving dinner to those who choose to follow her reasonable guidelines.

While an autocratic parent tries to tell the child what to do and a permissive parent lets the child tell him or her what to do, the democratic parent relies on choices and consequences as tools to help guide and influence the child toward responsible behavior. As Jason's mother becomes more skillful with these techniques, she will learn communication skills that will enable her to involve Jason more in the problem-solving process itself. In the meantime, she is off to a good start.

A Note on the Case Studies

You've now met the three families whose interactions we'll follow throughout the book. These families, though fictitious, are derived from many real families that I have worked with during the past dozen years. The problems and solutions are very real and serve to exemplify the skills and principles presented in Active Parenting. The family trees on the following page should help you keep the relationships straight in your mind.

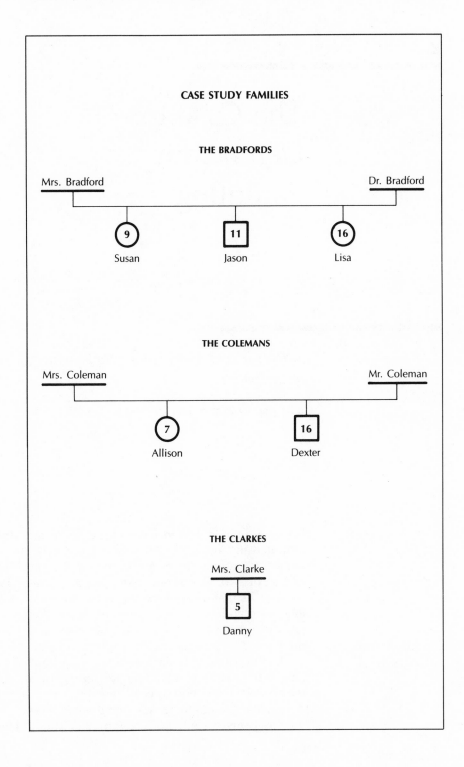

CASE STUDY FAMILIES

THE BRADFORDS

Mrs. Bradford   Dr. Bradford

9 Susan   **11** Jason   **16** Lisa

THE COLEMANS

Mrs. Coleman   Mr. Coleman

7 Allison   **16** Dexter

THE CLARKES

Mrs. Clarke

5 Danny

2

The Case for Democratic Parenting

A foolish consistency is the hobgoblin of little minds.

RALPH WALDO EMERSON

I have a definite bias in favor of the democratic style of parenting, as indicated in Chapter 1. And it's not just because I happen to like the democratic way of life and want to see it perpetuated for another generation or two. Democratic parenting is a down-to-earth, no-nonsense set of skills that works better than anything else in accomplishing both long-term and short-term parenting goals. And yet, most parents still use the autocratic style of parenting, because it's what they know: it's the style *their* parents used with *them*.

Do you know the story of the family lasagna recipe? Mother had taught the recipe to daughter for four generations, and always with the specific instruction to use a nine-by-twelve-inch pan. Finally, a ten-year-old girl thought to ask her mother, "Why do we always use a nine-by-twelve-inch pan?" Her mother didn't know, except to say,

"That's the way my mother taught me." So the little girl asked her grandmother, but *she* didn't know. Finally, the persistent little girl asked her great-grandmother, who sagely replied, "Because that was the only size pan I had."

The choice of a nine-by-twelve-inch pan was a good one for great-grandmother, but it was nonsense for the others. And so we laugh at this foolish consistency, and it makes a good joke. But like many good jokes, it also contains a piece of a mirror that reflects back a tiny bit of our own nonsense. Of course, not all consistency is nonsense. The world could not function without consistency. But when does a commonsense consistency become a foolish consistency? Usually when it stops working well, or otherwise blocks real progress.

Are you making a free choice as a parent regarding your parenting style? Or are you allowing others to determine it for you—others who lived in a different time and place and who had different goals for themselves and their children?

A Historical Context for Parenting

To fully understand the usefulness or uselessness of a specific tradition, it often helps to follow the little girl's approach and do some historical research. Let's take a firsthand look at the history of parenting as it parallels the history of freedom. As we take our trip through history, let's keep in mind these points:

1. If a parenting style no longer makes sense, we are free to change it.

2. As we have become a society of equals, democracy has replaced the old autocratic hierarchy.

Let's now trace some of the peaks and valleys of the Thor family history.

1,000,000 B.C., Thor's cave. Thor and son-of-Thor are huddled beside the fire where they've just invented the art of cooking. Father gives his son a burnt piece of woolly mammoth and says, "Ugh," which means, "Eat it. It's good for you."

His son takes a bite, then pushes it away, saying, "Ugh," which means, "I don't want it. It tastes funny."

Father then smashes son across the side of his head with a forearm the size of a redwood tree. Son reconsiders Father's offer, and says, "Ugh," which means, "You win; you're bigger; I'll do it your way."

FOOTNOTE: son remembers this lesson in power, and when he turns fifteen, he clubs his father into unconsciousness and takes over leadership of the clan.

So begins the "parenting-by-power" technique that is the hallmark of the autocratic parenting style. Brute force rather than common sense works well here, but as the society matures, it eventually—like our caveman's adolescent son—rebels and overthrows the oppressor.

A.D. *1215.* Lord Thorson, bloody well fed up with the way King James is running his life, joins his fellow nobles at Runnymead. King James signs the Magna Carta and suddenly an absolute hierarchy is less absolute.

That evening at dinner, the Thorson's son, William, asks, "Does this mean that all men are created equal? That they have a voice in those matters that affect their lives—a free will—an unalienable right to pursue happiness—freedom of speech?"

"Not for at least another 500 years," says his father. "Now go to your room, before I smack you!" Lord Thorson then coins the phrase, "Children should be seen and not heard."

1522. The feudal system is still going strong. Lady Thorson has explained to her three children the importance of knowing one's place. The oldest son demonstrates his understanding by bopping his younger brother on the head. His younger brother accepts the lesson gracefully and smacks his little sister. She, too, knows her place and goes outside to sock a peasant girl, who goes home and kicks a cat.

1775. Mr. Thorson, a resident of Boston, has just returned from a little tea party he and some other revolutionaries have thrown at the harbor. His prepubescent son, Max, is all ears as the patriots talk of freedom, liberty, and the movement by thirteen radical colonies for independence.

Max thinks how wonderful it must be to rebel for one's own rights. He thinks that maybe when he turns thirteen—like the colonies—he'll have enough power to rebel against "King" Thorson and proclaim his own independence. Mr. Thorson reads his son's mind and locks him in his room.

1865. Scarlett Thorson has just watched her Georgia plantation burn to the ground. The slaves are all gone, and the cotton is rotting in the fields. She wonders why the slaves left her after the Emancipation Proclamation was signed. Weren't they happy working in the fields sixteen hours a day without rights? Then she remembers the lake they were to put in for irrigation. "Rhett, honey," she calls to Mr. Thorson. "Will you put in the dam so we can have our lake?" "Frankly, my dear, I can't build a dam," replies her husband. Their fifteen-year-old son, Hoover, thinks about how wonderful it must be to be a freed slave as he is put to work building the dam.

1956. The members of the Thorson family of Atlanta are gathered around their newest acquisition, a television set. They have just turned off the news as Mr. Thorson asks his family, "What do you think of that Reverend King down in Montgomery and all this civil rights stuff?"

"I think it's high time Negroes were treated as equals with white folks," says a liberal Mrs. Thorson.

"Me, too," chimes in their ten-year-old daughter, Melanie.

"We studied the Declaration of Independence in school," adds her teenage brother, "and it says '*all* men are created equal.' "

"Very good," says Mr. Thorson proudly.

"Does 'all men' mean 'all women,' too?" asks Melanie.

"Let's watch *The Honeymooners,*" says Mr. Thorson, having just discovered a new use for TV.

1975. Melanie Thorson, a single parent living with her five-year-old son, Chad, has just returned from a feminist rally. She reflects momentarily on her ex-husband, Ted, and reassures herself that she is better off without him. She then hugs Chad, who has been watching TV with the sitter, and says, "How's my little boy doing?"

"Right on!" says Chad, repeating a catchy phrase he heard on the news.

"What's that?" asks his mom.

"Power to the people!" says Chad.

"Uh oh," says Ms. Thorson.

What can we learn from the Thorsons? That the historic movement by men and women toward equality has not completely bypassed our children. With no group a willing model of inferiority, today's children—ardent media consumers—have grown up believing that the phrase coined by Thomas Jefferson, "All men are *created* equal," really means at birth, not at age eighteen.

Fortunately, we are free to change our parenting style and avoid the sorts of rebellions that have plagued autocrats—whether kings or parents—throughout history. After all, in our democracy we *are* free to choose.

What Do You Mean, Kids Are Equal?

The idea that children now consider themselves our equals is difficult for many parents to accept. After all, we like to reason, they are so different. But before you reject this idea of equality completely, let's take a look at what the word *equal* really means.

Does *equal* mean "same"? No, it doesn't, and that's where much of the confusion exists. To be equal can also include to be different. For example, the dollar bill in my wallet and the dollar bill in yours are different in that they have different serial numbers, but they are of equal value. Even more different are a dollar and four quarters, or ten dimes. Yet, they all have the same value. So it is with people. Each of us is unique, and therefore different in many ways from each other, yet we live in a historical period that also entitles us to be treated as equals. The same can be said of our different races, religions, and sexes. The differences are a beautiful part of the human tapestry, but they do not preclude our equality.

Children are even more different and are in many ways *not* equal to parents. For example, we do not mean that children are their parents' equals in terms of *power*, for adults are bigger and stronger physically than most children, and adults have other kinds of social and economic power that are simply not available to most children. We also do not mean that children are their parents' equals in terms of *maturity*, for adults, unlike children, have had many years in which to develop their bodies, their minds, and their emotional stability. We do not mean that children are their parents' equals in terms of *roles*, for the parent's role is to be a leader in the family, while the child's role is to be a student or learner.

But what we *do* mean is that parents and their children are *social* equals. Children and adults have exactly the same claim to dignity and respect. The idea of social equality is new as applied to child rearing, but as we have seen, it has a long history in our culture. No longer are children willing to be subservient, to be seen and not heard, to follow parents' orders unquestioningly. We live in a society in which democracy and equality are ideals, and our children understand those ideals as well as we do.

A society of equals, like any other, must have leaders, but the leaders in a democracy are effective only when they use democratic techniques that are based on respect for those whom they lead. And so it follows that the leaders in the family—parents—need to use democratic techniques, and respect these social equals who are their own children. The old ways of parenting that worked for our parents and grandparents in another social atmosphere are not effective today. Because we are free men and women, and freedom is choice in decisions that affect our lives, it is up to us to *choose* a new style of parenting, a style that will have some of the elements of our parenting traditions, but that will be sufficiently different to be effective in our modern era.

In the 1950s, when educators and parents first began noticing that the old autocratic approach was losing its effectiveness, they made a radical—and unsuccessful—adjustment. The permissive style of the fifties and sixties was a reaction to the overbearing style of the autocrats. Children were expected to handle huge amounts of freedom and, given a loving environment, pretty much raise themselves. As with most reactive solutions, it backfired. Many children became self-indulgent, lacked responsibility, self-discipline, and motivation, and in fact rebelled at the lack of discipline and guidance. It is ironic that the stringent limits of the autocratic style *and* the neglect of limits of the permissive style both produced rebellious children.

The democratic approach—the parent as leader—has now emerged as a synthesis of the autocratic emphasis on limits and the permissive emphasis on freedom. This new emphasis on freedom *within* limits, coupled with a new respect for the child as a person, is the hallmark of democratic parenting. In fact, it is the hallmark of life in our democratic society itself. Let's take a closer look at why the democratic style has become the most effective approach in today's world.

The Purpose of Parenting

Over fifty years ago, Alfred Adler based a psychology, in part, on the idea that people are motivated more by their goals and purposes for the future than by so-called causes that lie in the past. Today, educators, psychologists, and motivational speakers all agree that defining our goals clearly is a key ingredient of success. To be successful parents, then, we need to develop an overall statement of purpose and to keep it in mind on a day-to-day basis. Let's do this together.

First, what is the basic goal of every living animal—including humans? To survive. And since infants and young children could never survive on their own, the first purpose of parenting is to protect our children.

How are human beings different from all the other animals? For one thing, we have the potential to do far more than merely survive. We can create art, music, literature, recreation, even spiritual awareness—we can, we might say, thrive. So the twin purposes of human beings are to survive and thrive. Because as parents we won't always be there to protect our children, we must also prepare them to survive and thrive on their own.

And where do we want our children to be able to survive and to thrive? If you saw the movie *Tarzan, the Legend of Greystoke*, you saw a powerful statement about the importance of taking into account the type of society in which a child will live. Here was a human infant raised in the jungle by apes as if he were their own child. They protected and prepared him so well to survive and to thrive that he eventually became the leader of all the apes. He had truly mastered the qualities necessary for thriving in that jungle society. But what happened when he was "rescued" and returned to the affluent British society? Not only was he unable to thrive, but his very survival was at risk. He was just not prepared for that society.

As parents, then, we want to prepare our children for life in the kind of society in which they live—in a high-tech democratic society, not in the jungles of Africa or the autocratic communist countries of Eastern Europe. So putting this all together, we have:

THE PURPOSE OF PARENTING

To protect and prepare our children to survive and to thrive in the kind of society in which they live.

Our next step is to ask, What kind of qualities will prepare our children best to survive and to thrive in a high-tech democratic society? The answer to that question will determine our goals for parenting.

What Kind of Children Are We Trying to Raise?

What qualities do you want to instill in your children? I once asked a family in their first counseling session what each member wanted from the rest of the family. When I got to the father, he looked me dead in the eyes and said, "Blind obedience."

What if we could instill an unquestioning obedience in our children? Would we want to? Would such obedience help a child to thrive in our democratic society—a society filled with choices and debates; a society in which individual responsibility and leadership are prized attributes? The obvious answer is no. A yes-man or yes-woman might survive in our society, but it is doubtful that he or she would thrive.

On the other hand, plenty of autocratic countries exist where having the courage to stand up for your own ideas can get you shot before dawn. Blind obedience might well be a useful quality in those societies, at least in terms of achieving the basic goal of survival. I would argue, however, that even under a dictatorship, blind obedience would not help a child to thrive. In countries where the qualities necessary to survive run counter to those that let a human being thrive, people are forced into a difficult choice. They can either abandon the idea of thriving and accept survival as the best they can do, or they can choose to risk their survival by working to create a society that's compatible with human development.

Fortunately, we do live in a society of equals. But if your child is going to succeed—to thrive—in *this* jungle, he or she is going to have to develop the qualities and skills to do so. Instilling such qualities may be a little tougher for parents than instilling blind obedience, but then again, we knew parenting required some sacrifices when we applied for the job.

Many qualities enable people to survive in a democracy, but three of them can be considered essential, and it is those that this book will teach you to instill in your child. Blind obedience, you may have guessed, is not one of them.

Courage is the first. Alfred Adler once said that if he could give only one gift to a child, it would be courage. If a child were courageous, he reasoned, that child could learn everything else that he or she needed to learn. Nurtured by parental guidance, children's courage enables them to try, to fail, to try again, until they master the challenges that life poses. With too little courage, children give up easily, or do not try at all. Fear that generates failure and failure that reinforces fear become a pattern that supports a lifelong attitude of regret and resentment. Courage is the foundation upon which children construct their personalities. It is the heart of the human potential.

Responsibility is the second quality that children need in order to thrive in a democracy. Rudolf Dreikurs, building on the foundation laid by Adler, stressed the importance of responsibility for individual growth and for survival. A democracy demands that its members make decisions and accept responsibility for the consequences of those choices. The reality of *our* society is that our children will be called upon to make thousands of choices, and they will be held *responsible* for their choices in that they will experience the consequences that follow. Some of these choices will involve life and death matters. Our children will be offered drugs; will they choose to accept? They will face choices about drinking, sex, crime, dropping out, and even suicide. They will have to choose how best to develop their talents, how they will earn a livelihood, and what ways they might help to create a wiser, more just society. And we, their parents, won't be there to tell them what to do. But if we have prepared them to make responsible decisions, and if we have instilled in them the courage to stand behind these decisions, then they will be equal to these challenges.

Cooperativeness is the third essential quality that we want our children to develop. In some circles, a great deal of emphasis has been placed on competition as the road to success. In reality, those individuals who have been aware of the magic of teamwork have always been the ones who have moved society forward. Helping children to learn that life is not a dependent, nor an independent, but rather an interdependent experience is a cornerstone of Active Parenting.

In a society of equals, cooperation skills have high value, and the child who can cooperate with others in whatever enterprise is far more likely to survive and thrive than one who has never learned how. In fact, the relationship between children and parents is ideally one of cooperation rather than conflict. But cooperation from children cannot be demanded; it must be won.

What About the Toys on the Floor?

Courage, responsibility, cooperativeness—these are noble qualities, and fostering them in our children is a high-minded purpose for parents to pursue. "BUT," I can hear you saying, "what about the mother whose son refuses to pick up his toys? Are you going to tell me how to get the toys picked up, or are you just going to philosophize for the entire book?!"

Good news, gentle reader. The time for philosophizing is almost over—the time for action soon to begin. But first, let's get something straightened out between us. I fully recognize that parents are people too. That *you* are a person. That like all persons you have goals and aspirations and dreams and constraints on your time and a strong desire to thrive in your own right. And furthermore, *you* deserve to thrive just as much as your child deserves to thrive. And for you, part of thriving may very well mean not having your living room look like a toy store after a tornado.

The challenge of modern parenting is this: to achieve your goals for yourself without doing harm to your child's development. "Development" in this case means developing the courage, responsibility, and cooperativeness necessary to thrive.

It may help to look at goals in two categories. Our long-term goals for our children are to develop such qualities as courage, responsibility, and cooperativeness. These goals take a long time to achieve (and, fortunately, a long time to destroy—a few bad experiences won't do it). But on a day-to-day basis, we deal with short-term goals, like teaching our children to put away their toys. The challenges of being a parent in this case is to teach this in such a way that we actually increase our children's responsibility, cooperativeness, and courage. To achieve our short-term goal (a neat living room) at the expense of these qualities not only robs our children of a useful learning opportunity, but also damages our own goal of a more harmonious relationship with our children. We'll see how this happens in Chapter 3 when we explore the dynamics of the parent-child relationship.

Does Everyone in the Democratic Family Get a Vote?

Does democratic parenting mean that everyone in the family gets a vote? No. Otherwise any family with three or more kids would end up living at Disney World.

This is going to sound like a hedge, but let's face it: democracy is a relative concept. We don't live in a *pure* democracy, where every issue is decided by the votes of everyone. We live in a *representative* democracy, where we have input into the decisions that affect our lives. We have a voice, a say. In fact, maybe the essence of democracy can best be summed up like this:

**Democracy doesn't mean that you will get your way;
it means that you will get your say.**

Perhaps this is why freedom of speech comes first in the Bill of Rights.

In a democratic family, parents are the leaders who make the decisions—sort of like Congress or the President—and they inevitably make some unpopular ones. Parents have to be able to enforce those decisions—sort of like the Justice Department. But our children, like us, ought always to have the right to let their leaders know how they think and feel, and have the opportunity to try and change their leaders' minds. And because your purpose as a parent is to instill in your children the qualities that will enable *them* to survive and thrive in a democracy, what better place to begin teaching democratic principles than in the family?

But what are the principles of a democracy? See if you agree with the understanding of the democratic process represented in the chart on page 30.

Principles of Democracy

PRINCIPLE	IN A DEMOCRATIC SOCIETY			IN A DEMOCRATIC FAMILY		
	YES	NO	COMMENTS	YES	NO	COMMENTS
Equality is a prized value.	√		*"all . . . are created equal."* The Declaration of Independence by Thomas Jefferson	√		Remember . . . "equal" does not mean "the same."
All citizens vote on everything.		√	The elected leaders do most of the decision making.		√	Parents are the leaders, and they, too, must make most decisions.
Citizens are free to do whatever they please.		√	There are limits to freedom, and consequences for breaking the laws set by the leaders . . . even *for* the leaders (that's equality again).		√	Again, there is "freedom within expanding limits." Even parents must accept some limits and abide by consequences.
All citizens have a voice and can influence the decisions of their leaders	√		Most elected leaders are highly sensitive to the opinions of their constituents.	√		Democratic parents listen to the opinions of their children, and allow them influence in family decisions.
Everyone can vote for who will lead		√	Only adults vote. Only citizens vote.		√	There are no voting booths in the womb. Children do not choose their parents.

3

Children:
On the Grow

It is not easy to be crafty and winsome
at the same time, and few accomplish
it after the age of six.

D. SUTTER

There is a story about a mother who had twin children. One of the children was outgoing and happy and always saw the bright side of life. The other, introverted and sad, always saw the negative. The mother did not understand her two children, and so she took them to see a child psychologist. After the initial visit, the psychologist proposed an experiment to see how far the differences between the children went. He put the sad, pessimistic child in a room filled with dozens of exciting toys. The other child, happy and optimistic, was put in a room knee-deep in horse manure. After thirty minutes, the psychologist went into the first room and found the little pessimist crying amidst his toys. "But I wanted a scooter and there isn't one!" He then

31

went into the second room where the child was happily digging through the manure. "Why are you so happy?" asked the psychologist. "Well," replied the little optimist, "with all this manure there just has to be a pony in here someplace, and I'm going to find it!"

Understanding children is often frustrating. When you were a child, did your parents ever indicate their frustration with you by saying these sorts of things?

- "I just don't understand you!"

- "Why do you do things like that?"

- "Where have I failed?"

Maybe they even uttered the parent's curse: "I hope when you grow up you'll have a child as bad as you!" Maybe they even got their wish, and you *are* as frustrated with your children as they were with you.

Understanding human behavior is a challenge, and understanding how and why children behave the way they do is a monumental challenge. If your parents did say things to you like the parent's curse, they were expressing their difficulty in understanding your behavior. After all, how did they know that you wanted a scooter—or were looking for a pony?

In this chapter and the next, I want to help you understand better how your children develop and why they behave as they do. With this knowledge, you will feel less frustrated during conflicts, and will recognize actions that you can take as a leader in the family. Then, in later chapters, we will build on this understanding as you learn specific methods of actively influencing your child's development.

How Children Develop

Newborn babies are small and helpless, and absolutely dependent on someone else for their survival—someone must feed, clothe, cuddle, and comfort them. How do such helpless creatures develop into independent adults with personalities of their own? Each of the many theories advanced on this subject has had to explain the relative importance of two variables in children's personality development: nature (our heredity) and nurture (our environment). In fact, the argument among psychologists over which factor is the more important has come to be called the nature-versus-nurture controversy.

Hereditary Factors

Some authorities believe that hereditary factors, transmitted from parents to children through genes and chromosomes, play a dominant role in the formation of children's personalities. This view holds that children's development is predetermined by the biological package with which they are born; physical, mental, and emotional aptitudes guide and tug the personality into shape.

These ideas are often transmitted through the folklore by such phrases as "bad blood" or "It's in his genes." In fact, most children are very tuned into the heredity theory—which is one reason why I always counsel divorced parents to avoid character assassination with each other. A child who repeatedly hears that his father is a "lazy no-good louse" will reason that since he has his father's blood in him, he must be destined to become a lazy no-good louse as well. Such reasoning is often unconscious, but many a louse has turned into lice through such assumptions and character attacks. It's much better to attack your ex-spouse's behavior—if you have to attack at all—and to leave his or her character alone.

Environmental Factors

Other authorities have believed that such influences as children's home surroundings, upbringing, nurturing, and experiences play the dominant role in shaping the personality. This view holds that children are passive entities whose development is shaped by outside influences and whose unique personalities are the result of these influences.

The folklore that supports this line of reasoning is heard in such phrases as "What do you expect—She came from a broken home," or the advertising slogan "Clothes make the man." Recently, environmental thinking has been seen in the exaggerated fear on the part of parents that children who experience sexual abuse are automatically scarred for life.

Children: Active or Passive?

While the heredity factor is dominant in such theories of personality as Sigmund Freud's psychoanalytic theory—with its emphasis on such biological urges as sex and aggression—the environment factor is the basis for the theories of behaviorists like B. F. Skinner, who argues that the environment—with its positive and negative reinforcements—actually *shapes* children's personalities much as a sculptor molds clay.

For all their differences, strong advocates of either hereditary *or* environmental factors have something very important in common. Both view children as more or less passive beings incapable of asserting the free will necessary to control the development of their personalities.

But another school of thought holds that while heredity and environment are important influences on personality, it is the way children *respond to* or *build with* these influences that determines the personality. In this view, children are not passive, but active. Children are not victims of heredity or circumstance, but are self-determining and creative, building a unique personality, perhaps without realizing it, by the way they respond—by the choices they make—in dealing with whatever influences come along. Children's destiny is not dictated by fate, but is a matter of choice. We are all responsible for who we are and what we do. This view was developed by Alfred Adler, a colleague of Freud's. As Adler pointed out, it is not what we *have* that is important, but what we *do* with what we have. History is filled with examples of individuals who have overcome difficult handicaps to lead satisfying lives and become contributing members of their communities.

The Building Blocks of Personality

Much of this book is based on the ideas of Alfred Adler, especially his view that individuals shape their own lives, building their own personalities by actively making use of the influences that come their way. We might think of these influences as building blocks that children use to construct a personality. Some of these building blocks are heredity, family atmosphere, family constellation, and parents' methods.

Heredity. As mentioned before, the biological package that children inherit from their parents is an important resource in building personality. Suppose, for example, that a young girl is taller than her peers; she could respond to that biological fact in many ways: by being proud of her height; by feeling awkward about it; by standing tall; by stooping; by trying to dominate smaller playmates; by trying to show them that she will *not* try to dominate them; by feeling physically uncoordinated; or by excelling at basketball. The way children respond to height, to appearance, or to any other physical characteristic, whether it be an asset or a handicap, is one of the many, many ingredients of personality.

Family atmosphere. For a small child, the family is the world. Almost all of the child's early environmental influences come from the family. Therefore, the kind of atmosphere that prevails in the family's day-to-day living really matters. What does it feel like to live in the home? Is there mutual respect and cooperation? Are family members' rights respected? Are the parents warm and caring? Is there good humor? Is there time for fun? Are girls "sugar and spice" and boys "rotten, made of cotton"? Whatever atmosphere prevails, the child will respond to it, and the responses could take any of hundreds of forms: optimism, pessimism, cheerfulness, timidity, curiosity, deceitfulness, belligerence, and on and on. The possible responses to the day-to-day atmosphere in the family world are endless, and children use them as building blocks in constructing personality.

Family constellation. Another influence to which the child cannot help but respond is the number of other children in the family, and whether the child is first, second, or last in birth order. Each family has its own unique configuration, and the role each individual chooses to play in that configuration is influenced by the way that person sees his or her position in the family. Most first children, youngest children, or middle children respond to their situations in characteristic ways that leave their mark on personality.

On page 36 is a chart showing some of those typical responses. The chart also shows some ways in which parents can avoid magnifying these characteristics. In using the chart, keep in mind that when a gap of more than five years exists between any two children, the effect is as if there were two separate families. *For example:*

- Lisa (sixteen) is treated as if an only child.

- Jason (eleven) is treated as if a first child.

- Susan (nine) is treated as if a second child.

As the chart shows, family constellation is another important building block for the child's personality. But what matters and makes a difference in the development of the child's personality is not so much the child's position in the family as his or her interpretation of that position. You and your children may or may not exhibit these typical characteristics, depending on the decisions you have made.

Methods of Parenting. The influence on children that parents have the most control over is their style of parenting. We have already discussed the three basic styles of parenting—autocratic, permissive, and democratic—and their implications in a modern society. So powerful is this building block that the only factor that can be considered more influential in a child's development is the child's own creative self.

This explains why even children who have experienced very negative parenting have been known to succeed and why children who have had the benefit of very positive parenting have been known to

Family Constellation Chart

POSITION	TYPICAL CHARACTERISTICS	IMPLICATIONS FOR PARENTS
First Child	■ Often takes responsibility for other siblings. ■ Gets along well with authority figures. ■ Likely to become a high achiever. ■ Needs to feel right, perfect, superior.	■ Avoid pressure to succeed. ■ Encourage the fun of participating, not the goal of winning. ■ Teach that "mistakes are for learning." ■ Show "how to be gentle with yourself" when accepting failure.
Only Child	■ Used to being the center of attention. ■ Unsure of self in many ways. ■ May feel incompetent compared to others (such as parents). ■ Likely to be responsible. ■ Often refuses to cooperate if fails to get own way.	■ Provide learning opportunities with other children. ■ Encourage visiting friends. ■ Have spend-the-night company. ■ Use child care and nursery schools.
Second Child	■ May try to catch up with older child's competence. ■ May try to be older child's opposite in many ways. ■ May rebel in order to find own place.	■ Encourage his or her uniqueness. ■ Avoid comparisons with oldest. ■ Allow second child to handle his or her own conflicts with the oldest.
Middle Child	■ May feel crowded out, unsure of position. ■ May be sensitive, bitter, or revengeful. ■ May be a good diplomat or mediator.	■ Make time for one-on-one activities. ■ Include in family functions. ■ Ask for his or her opinion.
Youngest Child	■ Often spoiled by parents and older siblings. ■ Often kept a baby. ■ Often self-indulgent. ■ Often highly creative. ■ Often clever.	■ Do not do for the youngest (especially on a regular basis) what he or she can do alone. ■ Don't rescue from conflicts (thus making a victim). ■ Don't refer to as "the baby." ■ Encourage self-reliance.

fail. As important as we are, we simply do not *control* our children's destiny; we *influence* it. The lives of our children are ultimately in their own hands.

What we can do by improving our own parenting skills is to improve the *probability* that our children will put their personality building blocks together in a successful way. And in our world without guarantees, probability is a very powerful force.

CASE 4

Lisa Bradford is typical in many ways of affluent suburban teenagers. She's more prep than punk, more into rock'n'roll than drugs, more interested in guys than in her homework, and she would rather be just about anyplace else than in her biology class. Her father, a successful doctor, finds it difficult to understand how anybody, let alone his own biological offspring, could have trouble with biology. How in the world she could have failed her first exam was beyond his understanding.

"I *hate* biology!" wailed Lisa. "Mr. Green is boring, and his test was so stupid!"

"Lisa, blaming Mr. Green for this F isn't going to change anything," responded her dad. "You're just going to have to study more if you're going to cut the mustard. Besides, biology is life. If you're tired of biology, you're tired of living."

"You're thinking of London, Dad. 'When you're tired of London, you're tired of life' is the quote. Biology is just a lot of worms in a petri dish and boring Mr. Green, who has the personality of a worm. It's not just me; all the kids say he's boring. I thought of the 'personality of a worm' part myself."

Dr. Bradford was not amused; after all, his first-born child had brought home an F in his favorite subject. "Lisa, I told you that you weren't studying enough and that this would happen. Now do you understand why I kept on you to do your reading?"

"I tried to read it," Lisa said, "but I couldn't concentrate. The book is as boring as Mr. Green."

"Now, look here, Lisa," said Dr. Bradford, now angry. "I've heard about as much complaining from you as I want to. You've got a good mind, young lady, but if you expect to get into a good college someday, you better start using it. Your nine-year-old sister has better study habits than you do, and it's showing up in her grades. It would for you, too, if you'd just try a little."

"Oh, shit," said Lisa as she slumped hopelessly into a bean-bag chair. "I hate worms."

Understanding Children's Behavior

Why is Lisa failing biology? Why is she resisting her dad's efforts to help? Why is her dad using this strategy to handle the situation? (For that matter, why is Mr. Green boring his students?) When we try to understand why people behave the way they do, we can look in two directions. We can look to the past and ask ourselves what *caused* the behavior, or we can look to the future and try to discover the *purpose* or *goal* of the behavior.

The notion of cause and effect is very practical when we are dealing with the physical world: with physics or chemistry or biology. In those disciplines, a given effect can clearly be shown to result from a given cause. But when we are dealing with the behavior of people, who are goal-oriented beings, things are different. Humans have the unique capacity to imagine a future and make choices about their behavior with that future in mind. In other words, human behavior is directed toward a purpose, and when we try to understand a child's behavior, it is more useful to ask, What is the *purpose* of this behavior? than What *caused* this behavior?

Why is Lisa failing biology? Her father, who looks at the F and asks, What *caused* it? can only conclude that a lack of study *caused* the poor grade. Though Lisa's poor studying habits may be a factor, this explanation provides little insight into the matter.

But let's ask the *purpose* of Lisa's F and see the possibilities unfold. Lisa's purpose might have been to show her father that she is her own boss and that he can't always get his way. Maybe his criticisms of her and his comparison of her to others hurt, and failing is a way to hurt him back (after all, he does value biology above all other courses). Or maybe the only way Lisa can get her dad's attention at all is to create a problem, and an F in biology achieves that purpose.

What is influencing Lisa to fail biology? We can't really say without knowing more about her relationship with her father. Keep in mind that most of our formulation of purposes and calculation of effects occurs without our awareness. Lisa is probably as unaware as her dad is of her purpose, yet it still exerts a powerful influence on her behavior. We can understand behavior better in general if we first strive to understand its purpose.

Our Purposes: Surviving and Thriving

We discussed the idea of surviving and thriving in Chapter 2, but let's briefly review it here in the context of understanding children's purposes. All animals, including human beings, are born with one overriding purpose: to survive. All other goals and purposes spring from this primary goal, and are secondary to it. But just what it takes to survive is different in different cultures, and in different stages of the human race's development. In very primitive times, when humans lived in caves and among other animals, life was marked by constant violence. Survival depended upon the ability to fight and kill, or else to run fast enough to escape danger. And survival of the human species depended upon the ability to reproduce at a rate fast enough to replace those who died off or were killed. It is no wonder that when Freud looked deep into the unconscious reaches of the human mind, he found sex and aggression lurking as primitive drives.

If survival is our *basic* purpose, what separates us from the lower animals is our human potential to move beyond merely surviving toward the growth and development of our spiritual, intellectual, social, and psychological selves. This unique human potential begs us to make meaning of our lives, to actualize our resources—in short, to thrive.

What does it take to survive and to thrive? Different psychologists have proposed three ingredients: belonging, learning, and contributing. These three goals can be seen as forming a spiral of development that can trend either upward or downward.

Our Developmental Goals: Belonging, Learning, Contributing

Freud's theory of primitive drives provided a basis from which some of his contemporaries developed and expanded ideas about human purposes. One of these contemporaries, Alfred Adler, noted that as we evolved, our ability to think and to reason opened up vast new possibilities for survival. Adler suggested that all human beings, of no matter what race, religion, or culture, share a common need to *belong*. Born into the world as a totally helpless being, a human baby cannot survive without the support of others. Children have an absolute need to *belong* to others, and so powerful is this early reality that the goal of *belonging*, of finding a place in the scheme of things, stays with us for life.

Comment: How is Lisa's F an attempt to belong? Several possibilities exist. A child who wants to find his or her unique place in the family sometimes feels that the family doesn't have room for two of a kind. Since nine-year-old Susan is the good student, maybe Lisa is striving to belong by being the bad one. We have already suggested another possibility—that failing biology is a way for Lisa to belong with her dad. And though it proves painful, negative attention is often preferable to no attention. Lisa may even sacrifice some belonging with her peers by failing (assuming they are passing the course) in order to reach her father.

Maria Montessori, an Italian educator who was also a contemporary of Freud's, contributed a second important idea to the discussion of what it takes to survive. She believed that *learning* is natural to human beings; we all naturally *want* to learn because our survival on the planet depends upon it. We cannot survive forever in total dependency on others; we must learn life skills—from the simplest to the most complex—in order to decrease our dependence on others and to stand on our own two feet. Thus, all human beings have basic and primitive needs *to belong* and *to learn*.

Comment: Lisa is obviously not pursuing her goal of learning in biology, but perhaps she has learned something about her father. Maybe she has learned how to get to him, how to show him how powerful she really is—powerful enough to make him angry and powerful enough to prevent him from making her study.

From the base of *belonging,* to the skills acquired through *learning,* children reach a point at which they can begin to contribute to the world as well as take from it. This is important for two reasons. First, only by the contributions of individual members to each other can our species survive and thrive. The world is just too tough on lone wolves. Second, the child's contributions enhance the sense of belonging, which in turn offers the secure base from which the child can attempt new learning.

Comment: Is Lisa contributing? Certainly not in a positive way. But in another sense she is playing her part in a power struggle with her father. She gives as well as takes as they go round and round in a deepening spiral. The result, however, is a loss of self-esteem for both, and a sense of defeat—what Lisa would call "a real downer."

However, children can also pursue their goals of belonging, learning, and contributing in positive ways. When this happens, an upward spiral begins, and children's self-esteem increases as their chances of surviving and thriving improve. The spiral might be pictured as a cylinder with *belonging, learning,* and *contributing* spiraling around the outside and upward toward the top.

In summary, then, here is how the surviving/thriving spiral works:

- Our basic purpose is surviving. Our potential purpose is thriving.

- Surviving and thriving are accomplished through three important goals:
  1. Belonging
  2. Learning
  3. Contributing

- *Belonging* leads to *learning,* which leads to *contributing,* which leads to *increased belonging.*

- This cycle is our way of moving from helplessness to surviving and thriving.

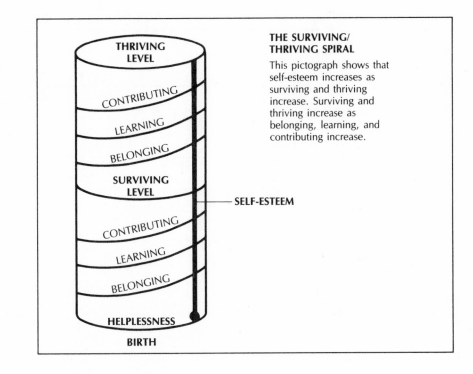

**THE SURVIVING/
THRIVING SPIRAL**

This pictograph shows that
self-esteem increases as
surviving and thriving
increase. Surviving and
thriving increase as
belonging, learning, and
contributing increase.

A Few Words About Encouragement

The surviving/thriving spiral can be thought of as the underlying heart-beat of children's development. The elements of this cycle—belonging, learning, and contributing—form a lifelong process that flows out of children's early life experiences. When children can find positive ways of belonging, learning, and contributing, they gain the self-esteem and courage that enable them to tackle the problems that life offers. Such children, we say, feel *encouraged*.

The chart on page 42 shows some of the ways that parents can encourage their children to reach their goals of belonging, learning, and contributing. There are blank spaces at the bottom of each list so that you can write down other ways that occur to you.

But the opposite can also occur. When children feel that they cannot belong through positive means; when children's attempts to learn are squelched and their contributions rejected, self-esteem decreases, and children feel *discouraged*. We will see the results of such discouragement in the next two chapters, and then deal with the important topic of encouragement in Chapter 6.

Ways to Help Children Reach Their Goals

BELONGING	LEARNING	CONTRIBUTING
Hold	Teach skills	Accept their offers of help
Touch	Encourage self-reliance	Ask for their help
Hug	Provide opportunities	Ask for their opinions
Kiss	Avoid too much criticism	Express appreciation for their efforts
Love	Accept mistakes	Share responsibilities with them
Play	Show interest in their knowledge	Acknowledge their cooperation
Invite	Continue your own learning	Offer them your help

4

When Children
Misbehave

*Insanity is hereditary—you get it from
your children.*

SAM LEVENBURG

Children misbehave in two ways: when they "don't know any better,"
and when they do. It's the latter category of misbehavior that tends to
drive parents crazy.

When a child "doesn't know any better"—for example, when a
three-year-old belches at the dinner table—we are quick to assume our
role as leader and educator in the family as we offer guidance in a firm
and friendly manner. We graciously accept the responsibility of preparing our child for thriving in our civilized society. After all, the child
may be at a State Department dinner someday, and belching at the
wrong time could be a political disaster. So we lovingly inform our
child that "when we burp like that, honey, we cover our mouth like
this, and say 'excuse me.' " We might even let the child try it, and then

praise the results. Yes, when children don't know any better it brings out the best in their parents.

But what happens when that three-year-old's ten-year-old brother, who has just witnessed this episode in active parenting, lets loose five minutes later with a belch that registers on the Richter scale? Are we as calm and understanding? Of course not, because he "knows better." We recognize that he is up to something, and perhaps take it as a personal affront or challenge of our authority.

But are the two types of misbehavior really that different? Both children are exploring their worlds—wondering how much freedom they have and where the limits really are. In the first case, the three-year-old may have no idea where the limits are regarding mealtime expulsions, so she is using a trial-and-error method to find them. Her ten-year-old brother, however, knows exactly where the limits are, but he too is exploring—looking for answers. How firm are these limits? Are they always there? When aren't they really there (that is, When can I get away with it?)? And most important, what will happen if I go beyond these limits? What are the negative consequences and what are the payoffs?

Once big brother gets this information, he will truly "know better." Will he then stop this particular misbehavior? That depends on whether or not the misbehavior helps him achieve his goals. If it does, he is likely to repeat it later. If not, he will look for other ways to achieve these goals. Kids just won't do what doesn't work.

Since misbehavior is related to attaining goals and since children's goals usually relate to their parents, parents would benefit from knowing what these goals are. Fortunately, we have some very accurate information about goals of children's misbehavior. But before we discuss these goals (and learn how to recognize them), it will be useful to look at their roots—the *basic* goals of children's behavior.

The Four Immediate Goals of Children's Behavior

The three goals that form the surviving/thriving spiral (belonging, learning, contributing) can be thought of as the undercurrent that runs through the stream of human development. On a daily basis, however, we find it more practical to consider four other goals that exist closer to the stream's surface: contact, power, protection, and withdrawal.

Contact. Out of our desire to belong, each of us develops the goal of making contact—physical or emotional—with other human beings. An infant's need to be held is actually critical to his or her survival. Later, the child learns other forms of contact: touch, communication, attention, and recognition. Even adults (or perhaps *especially* adults) have strong needs for contact with other human beings—the existence of clubs, parties, friendships, and marriage attests to this hunger. Everyone wants to be regarded as a person in his or her own right—to receive the recognition and the affirmation that come from the respect and affection of others.

Power. Each of us wants to influence our environment and gain at least a measure of control over it. We would like things to go our way; we want the power to make that happen. It is through learning that we become able to do this; as the saying goes, "Knowledge *is* power." And as parents, we want to encourage children to develop their power, and eventually to learn to use it to make positive contributions.

Protection. To survive and thrive we must be able to protect ourselves and our families. Our instinctive desire to repel attacks—whether physical or psychological—has led to the development of elaborate systems of justice and defense. Yet, it is through contributing that our self-protection reaches its highest point. When we help our neighbor survive and thrive, our neighbor is less likely to become desperate and to attack us. Thus, our own protection is enhanced.

Withdrawal. Time-outs are essential and refreshing in any sport. A child who seeks contact also needs, at other times, to withdraw, regroup, center. Again, our early survival instinct taught us to withdraw from danger; and withdrawing counterbalances the goal of contact.

The concept of these four goals of human behavior originated in the work of Rudolf Dreikurs, an Adlerian psychiatrist whose book *Children: The Challenge* has been the single most important contribution to the field of parent education. Dreikurs's famous four goals of misbehavior form the basis of my own treatment of understanding children's misbehavior. Don Dinkmeyer and Gary D. McKay, authors of the STEP program, expanded Dreikurs's model to describe four companion goals of children's positive behavior.

"Encouraged" Behavior and "Discouraged" Behavior

What Dreikurs and Dinkmeyer called "goals," however, might better be thought of as approaches to reach the basic goals that we have just discussed:

■ contact

■ power

■ protection

■ withdrawal

Why do children sometimes approach these basic goals in positive ways and at other times by misbehaving? Why do some children often choose positive approaches while others seem to choose the approaches of misbehavior?

I would like to suggest to you that there are no *good* or *bad* children, but only *encouraged* or *discouraged* children, whose behavior is more or less useful or useless. In other words, a child who feels encouraged is likely to pursue each of the basic goals with behavior that parents would call positive; a child who feels discouraged, on the other hand, is likely to pursue the same goals with what might be called negative behavior. The following chart illustrates these differences.

BASIC GOAL	ENCOURAGED CHILD'S APPROACH	DISCOURAGED CHILD'S APPROACH
Contact	Seeking recognition	Seeking undue attention
Power	Showing independence	Rebellion
Protection	Being assertive, extending forgiveness	Seeking revenge
Withdrawal	Centering	Avoidance

Let's look at some specific cases to see how children are encouraged or discouraged in their approaches to the four goals.

CASE 5

When I first met Allison Coleman and her parents, they were quick to point out that they had not always been so annoyed by her behavior. In fact, until about a year before we met, they had considered her quite a pleasure. She was always willing to help out around the house—in fact, she often offered. Unfortunately, there were very few jobs that her mother felt Allison was big enough to handle, and so she would often send Allison along to play and do the job herself.

Now it seemed that Allison was always there—like a shadow. Her mother described her annoyance one morning, for example, when she was on the telephone. Every minute or two Allison interrupted. First, it was to show her a picture she had painted. "Do you like this color?"

she asked. Then it was to ask when lunch would be ready; then to ask where her favorite jersey was; then to ask, "What time is it, Mommy?" Mrs. Coleman patiently answered each question, but was clearly getting irritated.

Comment: This case offers us an example of a child pursuing the basic goal of contact. In her earlier years, Allison pursued this goal with a positive approach. She sought recognition by offering to help with the household chores. Her mother's repeated rejection of such offers became discouraging, however, and Allison eventually turned to seeking undue attention. She has skillfully developed a number of positive as well as negative means of getting the contact from her mother she craves.

CASE 6

We've already met Danny Clarke and his single mother. Remember his refusal to pick up his toys and come to dinner? Remember his mother's autocratic, heat-seeking-missile approach to his backside? The frustration and anger that she felt are the typical negative feelings generated from this type of power struggle. Both Danny and his mom are pursuing their goals of power—each rebelling against the other's demands. Danny has gone beyond independence, and through rebellion is trying to show his mother that he can't be bossed around. Mother, equally strong-willed (and probably at one time a rebellious child herself) is out to show her son that she is the boss. Their power struggle ends in a stalemate that will be repeated again in other situations.

CASE 7

Dexter Coleman (age sixteen), Allison's big brother, has everything going for him. He's a good student, popular, gets along well with his parents, and has already made the varsity basketball team. And Dexter has a positive approach to the basic goal of protection.

Like many little sisters, Allison used to come into Dexter's room without permission. One time, she accidentally broke a model that he was working on for a science project. Of course, he was angry, but rather than clobber Allison, he took it up with the whole family at a family council meeting. The family decided that Allison would pay for the broken model by selling one of her toys at their garage sale. Dexter didn't hold a grudge, but he did begin locking his breakable possessions in the closet.

Comment: Because Dexter has a good sense of self-esteem, he takes an encouraged approach to protection. He neither lets Allison take advantage of him nor does he blindly seek revenge. Rather, he looks for ways to correct the wrong and prevent it from happening again. He is also willing to forgive.

CASE 8

In addition to Lisa, Jason Bradford has a second sister, Susan. While Lisa, the oldest, gets many privileges that Jason can only hope to attain when he is a teenager, Susan gets the special attention that often flows to "the baby," so Jason often feels squeezed in the middle. To compound matters, Dr. Bradford often has excessively high standards for his only son and is frequently critical. Jason's discouragement has led to resentment and a negative approach to protection.

Dr. Bradford is particularly concerned about his son's lying. For example, Jason recently had a book report due on Monday. On Sunday night, when Jason sat down to watch a movie on TV, his father asked if the report was ready to be turned in the next day. Jason said yes and his dad let it go at that. A few days later, Susan told her father that Jason had gotten into trouble at school for not handing in the report. Dr. Bradford was angry, and he confronted Jason, who yelled "I hate you!" and ran out of the room. Dr. Bradford felt hurt both by Jason's words and his lying, and he punished Jason by grounding him for the weekend. Jason went out on his bike for two hours Saturday afternoon anyway, and socked Susan on the arm for telling. His dad was furious.

Comment: When a child takes a revengeful approach to protection, we can be sure that he has felt hurt himself and is seeking to get even. Unfortunately, attempts at revenge usually backfire, as Dr. Bradford and Jason have demonstrated, when they lead to retaliation and an escalation of hurt feelings. Dr. Bradford's own hurt feelings tell us that Jason's approach is to seek revenge—to hurt someone for a real or imagined wrong. By punishing Jason, Dr. Bradford just hurts him more and provokes revenge—and more retaliation.

Susan, meanwhile, is playing a little game of "let's you and he fight." By telling on Jason she makes herself look good by getting him into trouble. Then when Jason seeks revenge by socking her arm, she can tattle again. By playing this game with her, her father unwittingly increases Jason's desire for revenge and teaches Susan how to be a victim.

CASE 9

You probably recall from Chapter 3 Lisa's conversation with her father about her biology grade. Following that frustrating and discouraging encounter with her dad, Lisa made a halfhearted effort to pass her next exam. Fortune smiled and she came up with a D. Dr. Bradford, however, didn't smile, and in fact told her, "I guess I'm just wasting my time with you." His disgust was apparent. Meanwhile, Lisa didn't have a date for an important dance, and she felt that her life was falling apart on all fronts. Her mother noticed Lisa spending more time alone in her room, but she, too, felt helpless about the situation.

Comment: Lisa's level of discouragement is so high that she seeks to avoid any further pain, humiliation, or failure. She may soon stop trying altogether. Dropping out of school, turning to drugs, or even attempting suicide are all within the realm of possibility. In such cases, massive encouragement by the parents, a coordinated effort with the school, and even professional counseling are often necessary to intervene in the discouragement process. Sometimes the avoidance approach is more temporary, and the child may be able to work it out with a little assistance and a lot of encouragement.

The Four Mistaken Approaches and How to Handle Them

When you are confronted by a child's misbehavior, you will understand that behavior better if you ask yourself, What is the goal of this behavior? There are two guidelines to help you determine what the child's goal really is. The first guideline is *your own feeling* about the behavior: Is it irritation, anger, hurt, or helplessness? The second guideline is *the child's response* to your reaction, for the child's response is likely to be different with each of the differing goals.

Seeking Undue Attention

The mistaken idea behind seeking undue attention is that children do not count unless they have an adult's attention. So children find ways to keep adults' attention. Children may act forgetful, or helpless, or lazy, getting negative attention as their parents remind or coax them. Or children may get attention by clowning, asking constant questions, pestering, or becoming a nuisance.

The parent's usual response to this behavior is *irritation*. And if the parent expresses the irritation, the child's response is usually predictable: the child will stop the attention-getting behavior temporarily, but start it up again and continue it as long as it achieves the goal of getting the parent's attention.

What can you do? If you react to your child's negative attention-seeking behavior by giving attention, unwillingly and with irritation, by explaining, reminding, or nagging, you will be giving exactly the reaction that the child is seeking. To change this, you can do these things: ignore the irritating behavior; remove yourself from your child if necessary. Give your child your full attention at unexpected times; this will be encouraging and will direct your child's efforts to the positive side of the goal of contact. Show your child that he or she can belong by making useful contributions rather than bids for your service. Finally, use logical consequences as a discipline tool to teach your child the limits of attention seeking. (We will discuss the use of logical consequences in Chapter 8.)

CASE 5 (ALTERNATIVE)

The first time Allison interrupted her mother while she was on the telephone, her mother could say in a firm and friendly voice, "Allison, I'm on the phone; I will talk to you as soon as I am finished." An even better idea would be to set the kitchen timer for a specific length of time (say ten minutes) and tell Allison, "It will be your time to talk to me when the buzzer sounds in ten minutes." She could then ignore any further interruptions, giving Allison her *full* attention after the call was finished. If Allison's interruptions escalated to the point that her mother could not continue her conversation, she could excuse herself from the phone and give Allison a choice. For example, she could say, "Allison, you may either play in here quietly until I'm done or you may play in your room; you decide, dear." If Allison continued to interrupt, she could be taken firmly to her room. Mrs. Coleman's friend would understand the need to take time for teaching Allison limits.

Rebellion

Children who seek power over their parents operate under the mistaken notion that they count only when they are in control, or when they are winning as opposed to cooperating. Children may throw temper tantrums to get parents to give in, or may be stubborn and refuse to do what is asked. Sometimes children get their own way by devious means. The parent who does not give in will perhaps fight.

The usual parental response to rebellious behavior is *anger*. And if the parent begins to join in a power struggle with the child, the child's usual response is to intensify the behavior, redouble the efforts to gain power, and escalate the struggle. The parent's anger and display of force make it more important than ever for the child to "win."

What can you do? You can avoid reacting as your child expects. The key is to neither fight nor give in. You can defuse the situation with a firm but friendly action, by removing yourself from the conflict. An argument cannot continue if one side stops talking, nor can a physical fight continue if one side leaves the arena. You must, however, resolve to understand what the power struggle is about and to constructively interact with your child as soon as everyone has cooled down. During that time you can talk about alternative solutions or agreements as to how each of you will behave in the future. In a later chapter, we will discuss how to deal with problems of this kind.

CASE 6 (ALTERNATIVE)

To handle Danny's rebellion, Mrs. Clarke could first recognize that her son's refusal to come to dinner is a challenge to a power struggle. If she fights *or* gives in she has accepted the challenge and lost the battle. How could she sidestep Danny's rebellion and neither fight nor give in? She could decide what *she* would do. First, she could give Danny some advance warning about when dinner would be ready. Again, a kitchen timer works wonders. "Danny, can you set the timer for five minutes? That's when dinner will be ready." If he did not come when the timer buzzed, she could give him a choice. For example, she could say, "Danny, do you want to eat dinner now and play with video games afterward or should I put the video away until tomorrow?" She might also let Danny choose to miss dinner that night. "Do you want to come to dinner or should I put it away and you can eat next at breakfast?" In either case, she should remain friendly while she enforced Danny's choice. We will discuss these methods more fully in Chapter 8.

Seeking Revenge

An escalation of the power struggle usually leads children to seek revenge, especially if they feel the parent has "won" too many battles, or has hurt them in some other way. Children then feel that the best form of protection is to hurt back, to return punishment for punishment in an attempt to get even. In an illogical way, children feel that revenge equalizes things in their world.

The parent's usual response to this behavior is to feel *hurt*. The parent may even dislike the child, and wonder how he or she could be so hurtful. If the parent attempts punishment, the child will generally escalate the misbehavior.

What can you do? Once again, withdraw from the emotionally charged situation and avoid the temptation to hurt back. Refuse to allow yourself to be hurt, by avoiding the situation both physically and emotionally. Resolve to interact positively with your child during neutral times, and to establish logical consequences for misbehavior, should it recur. In Chapter 8, we will discuss the positive value of establishing natural and logical consequences for misbehavior.

CASE 8 (ALTERNATIVE)

To deal with Jason's revenge-seeking behavior, Dr. Bradford could first recognize that Jason also feels hurt, and seek to understand what he feels hurt about. He could share *his* hurt feelings with Jason without resorting to anger and escalation. He could say, for instance, "Jason, when I found out that you lied to me about the book report, I felt pretty hurt. I wonder—for you to have hurt me—maybe there are some things that I've done that have hurt you?" He could explore this with Jason and perhaps discover some things they might both agree to do differently. Dr. Bradford could also focus on building the positive side of their relationship using the family enrichment skills found in Chapter 7.

Avoidance

Extremely discouraged children give up, become passive, and refuse to try anything. Such children may assume disabilities in order to avoid parental expectations. An "I can't" attitude becomes a defense that enables discouraged children to avoid trying, and therefore to avoid the risk of further failures. Such children feel like failures at everything, so have the attitude that no one should expect anything from them.

The parent's usual response to this behavior is a feeling of *helplessness*. Parental attempts to get the child to "give it a try" are often met with increased resistance or passivity.

What can you do? You can be patient, accepting of your child, and encouraging. Remind yourself that your child is probably exaggerating his or her own assumed disability in order to see whether the worst could be true (that is, whether the child is as bad off as he or she claims to be). Give your child small tasks under the assumption that he or she will succeed. Look for tasks that you know he or she can do, and let your child enjoy the flush of success and the consequent encouragement that comes from doing them.

CASE 9 (ALTERNATIVE)

To handle Lisa's avoidance, Dr. Bradford could first recognize his own contribution to the problem. By being perfectionistic and critical, he adds to Lisa's discouragement. He could recognize that Lisa need not succeed in biology (or even high school) to be a worthwhile person who deserves his love and respect. He could learn to appreciate her strengths and develop the skills that would encourage her to grow. He could also work with Lisa to arrange a meeting at school of the people involved. If the problem continued, he and his wife could consult a family therapist.

The ABCs of Behavior

My emphasis, thus far, on understanding children's misbehavior has been to recognize their basic goals and mistaken approaches. Goals are beliefs, and approaches are actions. But what about feelings, and how do other people's actions influence us? If we can put the relationship between beliefs, feelings, and actions together in a useful way, it will become much clearer how we influence our children and how they influence us.

Albert Ellis, a contemporary psychologist, has developed a helpful model for understanding this relationship. He began by observing that most people act as if other people controlled or caused their feelings. Such phrases as "you made me angry" or "you make me happy" underscore the attitude that others determine our feelings for us.

We can look at this schematically by letting "A" represent the "activating event" and "C" represent the "consequent feeling." When Danny refused to come to dinner and his mother became angry (Case 1), it would have been easy for his mother to say, "Danny made me angry . . ."

A→C

The truth is that although other people do *influence* or *trigger* our feelings, the *cause* of our feelings is our own beliefs, attitudes, and values. Great thinkers have known this for centuries. For example, the

BASIC GOAL OF CHILD'S ACTION	ENCOURAGED OR DISCOURAGED CHILD'S APPROACH TO GOAL	CHILD'S BELIEF	PARENT'S TYPICAL FEELING	CHILD'S RESPONSE	SOME ACTIONS YOU CAN TAKE
Contact	*Encouraged:* Recognition	My contributions are recongnized. I belong by cooperating. I enjoy human contact.	Closeness	Cooperation and contribution.	Encourage cooperation; acknowledge the child's contributions.
	Discouraged: Undue attention	I belong only when I'm noticed or served. The world must revolve around me.	Irritation	Stops, but begins again very soon.	Ignore the behavior. Give the child full attention at other times. Use logical and natural consequences; act, don't talk.
Power	*Encouraged:* Independence	I am able to influence what happens to me. I am responsible for my life.	Admiration	Responsible, self-motivated behavior, learning.	Give responsibilities. Continue to encourage.
	Discouraged: Rebellion	I belong only when I'm the boss or when I'm showing you that you can't boss me.	Anger	Escalates behavior or gives in only to fight again another day.	Remove yourself from the conflict. Talk about it after the cooling-off period. Don't fight and don't give in. Take sail out of wind.
Protection	*Encouraged:* Assertiveness, forgiveness	When attacked or treated unfairly, I can stand up for myself and those I love. I am able to forgive and even contribute to those who have wronged me.	Love	Positive contact.	Express your own positive feelings; demonstrate assertiveness and forgiveness in your own relationships.
	Discouraged: Revenge	I've been hurt and will get even by hurting back. Then maybe they'll learn they can't get away with hurting me!	Hurt	To continue to hurt, or to escalate misbehavior.	Refuse to be hurt. Withdraw from the conflict. Show love to vengeful child. Avoid temptation to hurt back.
Withdrawal	*Encouraged:* Centering	There are times when I need to be alone. And there are situations to be left alone.	Respect	Resumes contact when ready.	Respect the child's wishes to be alone. Don't press. Later, use Active Communication.
	Discouraged: Avoidance	I'm a failure at everything. Leave me alone. Expect nothing from me.	Helplessness	Becomes passive; refuses to try; gives up.	Be patient; find ways to encourage child.

ACTION PAGE 3

Using the chart on page 54, practice identifying the mistaken approach and the basic goal of each of the following misbehaviors.

1. Susan (age ten) is lying in bed reading a comic book. Her dad tells her that she should be getting ready for school. Susan ignores him and keeps reading. Five minutes later, her father tells her again. She says okay, but makes no effort to get ready. Her dad comes in a third time and is very angry. He tells her to get dressed this instant or she's getting a spanking.

Susan's mistaken approach: _____

Basic goal: _____

2. The situation is the same, but this time when Susan's father tells her to get dressed, she puts down the comic book and does begin. But two minutes later she gets distracted by another comic book, and sits down on the bed reading again. Her dad reminds her of the time, and she continues dressing. A little later she has turned on the TV and still isn't ready. Her father is annoyed, but continues to coax.

Susan's mistaken approach: _____

Basic goal: _____

3. Susan says she doesn't want to go to school today. Her father tries to encourage her, but Susan seems very down in the dumps. A little later she admits that she hates school and is failing three subjects. Susan's father feels helpless in trying to motivate her.

Susan's mistaken approach: _____

Basic goal: _____

4. This time when Susan's father tells her to get ready, she yells at him, "Get off my back!" He tells her not to talk to him that way, but she calls him an ignorant jerk. He blows his stack and slaps Susan across the face. She buries her head in her pillow sobbing, "I hate you! I hate you!" Her father leaves dejectedly, hurt by her words.

Susan's mistaken approach: _____

Basic goal: _____

5. Write down a conflict from your own family. Tell what happened and how you felt.

Your child's mistaken approach: _____

_____

Basic goal: _____

ANSWERS

1. Susan's dad's *anger* and her *noncompliance* indicate a power struggle. Her mistaken approach: *rebellion*. Basic goal: *power*.

2. Susan's dad's *annoyance* and her *start-stop* response indicate a mistaken approach of *seeking undue attention* and a basic goal of *contact*.

3. Susan's dad's *helplessness* and her *unwillingness to try* suggest a mistaken approach of *avoidance* and a basic goal of *withdrawal*.

4. Susan's dad's *hurt* feelings and her *escalation* of the conflict indicate *seeking revenge* and a basic goal of *protection*.

Greek philosopher Epictetus said, "Men are not disturbed by things, but by the view they take of things." That one's point of view is critical has also been expressed by Shakespeare, who wrote, "There is nothing either good or bad but thinking makes it so." We can represent the belief that comes between the activating event A and the consequent feeling C as B (for belief). The relationship then becomes

A→B→C

which means an event triggers our belief system, which causes our feeling.

Since we actually cause our own feelings—through our conscious and unconscious beliefs, attitudes, and values—it stands to reason that we should accept responsibility for what those feelings are. To blame them on others is not only incorrect, it also reduces our power and self-control. In effect, when Danny's mom says, "You make me angry," she is saying, "You control my feelings." Since Danny's goal is power, and he is seeking power via the mistaken approach of rebellion, his mother's statement actually reinforces his rebellion. He says to himself, "Look how powerful my rebellion is; I made this big person loose her temper!"

However, when we accept responsibility for our own feelings, we actually increase our power and influence in a given situation. The voice of our responsibility says, "I have a choice: I can either get angry or I can take some other action to resolve the problem." This puts us back in control of ourselves. When we push our own buttons instead of giving away that power, we have many alternatives available to us. By choosing a different attitude or belief, we not only affect our feelings, but our likely actions (D) as well.

WHO'S IN CONTROL	ACTIVATING EVENT (A)	BELIEF (B)	FEELING (C)	ACTION (D)
Child in control	Danny refuses to come to dinner.	"Kids shouldn't rebel. I must make him mind."	Anger	Screech and hit
Parent in control	Danny refuses to come to dinner.	"Danny is rebelling; I don't need to fight or give in."	Determination	Present child with choices and enforce logical consequences.

Even if we don't change our beliefs to the extent that our feelings change, by expressing responsibility for these feelings (A→B→C), we maintain more power and are less likely to reinforce a child's rebellion.

STATEMENT	MODEL	WHO GETS THE RESPONSIBILITY AND THE POWER?
"You make me angry!"	A → B	Child
"I'm angry that you didn't come when I called."	A → B → C	Parent

The Parent-Child Behavior Cycle

We can use our understanding of children's goals and the ABCs of feelings to better understand how parents and children influence each other. The purpose of understanding these dynamics is to learn how to more effectively influence our children. We are always influencing each other, but we often inadvertently influence our children to continue misbehaving. Our behavior—what we do to correct the misbehavior—is the key. This action, you recall, is labeled D in the schema.

For example, when Danny refuses to come to dinner (A), because of her beliefs about obedience (B) his mother becomes angry at Danny (C), and yells and spanks him (D). But as you are well aware, the situation doesn't end with Mrs. Clarke's behavior—whether it's a spanking or anything else. What happens is that her behavior (D) becomes another activating event (A) for Danny, who begins an A-B-C-D cycle of his own.

For example: Danny's mom yells and spanks him (Danny's A).

■ Danny *believes*, "This is unfair, but look how powerfull I am" (Danny's B).

■ Danny *feels* angry too (his feeling C).

■ Danny says, "I hate you" (his behavior D).

And Danny's behavior (D) then becomes the next activating event (A) for his mother's A-B-C-D cycle. The cycle goes on and on until the two of them physically separate. This is why Dreikurs recommended that parents remove themselves from the power struggle.

Look at a diagram of the entire parent-child cycle on page 58. Remember, since it is a cycle, it does not matter where you begin; each step influences all the others.

Again, remember that change at any point in the cycle eventually filters throughout the cycle. This means that we can influence our children in many ways—and they can influence us in many ways. In the chapters ahead, you will be developing skills that will help you influence your children to choose positive approaches in pursuing their basic goals.

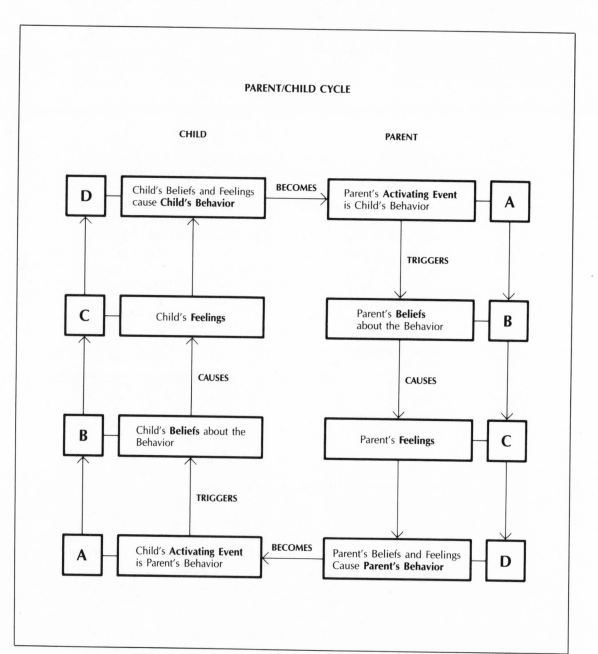

5

When Parents Misbehave

The real menace in dealing with a five-year-old is that you begin to sound like a five-year-old.

JEAN KERR

The title of this chapter may have surprised you. But you were probably no more surprised than the children to whom I once posed this question: "What do you do when your parents misbehave?" We are generally not used to thinking in terms of parents misbehaving. But since parents are humans and since all humans make mistakes, some of our behavior is mistaken behavior or what we typically call *mis*behavior.

When parents misbehave, their children respond to that mistaken behavior—often with mistaken behavior of their own. As we saw, mistaken behavior is one way children can approach their basic goals of contact, power, protection, and withdrawal. What causes them to take the mistaken approaches of seeking undue attention, rebellion, seeking revenge, and avoidance? Their beliefs and feelings—specifically, beliefs and feelings of discouragement. Where does this discouragement originate? Sometimes in the mistaken behavior of their parents. We call this parental misbehavior discouragement because it actually deprives children of courage. Without the courage to pursue their basic goals positively, children turn to the easier, negative approaches—misbehavior.

Most parents do not intend to discourage their children. In fact, as parents we are often unaware that our behavior *is* discouraging. Our intention is actually to encourage or motivate, but mistakes happen and we miss our mark. Sometimes we miss it because we lack information—we just have not been taught how children think and what is likely to be discouraging. In other words, we don't know any better.

At other times, we do know better. As soon as we open our mouths, we know that what we are about to say will be hurtful and discouraging. But we are frustrated, angry, tired—and so we go ahead and misbehave. Sometimes we even have the strange experience of hearing our own parents' discouraging words coming out of *our* mouths. The very same words we once vowed that we would never use on our children come pouring down like acid rain on the heads of our offspring.

The purpose of this chapter is to help you learn to recognize some of the common ways parents discourage their children—to help you *know* better. The purpose of the next chapter, as well as the remainder of the book, is to help you *do* better. As you read about the ways parents misbehave, try to be aware of your own lapses. Self-awareness is a powerful motivator, but only if you refrain from blame and self-punishment. Remember the affirmation from Chapter 1; no parent is perfect, nor is perfection the goal. And any amount of discouragement can be corrected in the future. First we work to reduce the discouragement, *then* to increase the encouragement. Also remember that the misbehaving child is always a discouraged child. Children who believe that they cannot find their place in the family by behaving properly will try to find their place by misbehaving.

Courage Is the Key

There was a little boy who was afraid of the dark. He lived in a time before the proliferation of convenience stores, when milk was still delivered to the door. Early one morning while it was still dark outside, the boy's mother asked him to bring in the milk. He was afraid. But his mother reassured him, saying, "It's okay, honey, God's outside.

He'll protect you." The little boy seemed to gain confidence as he looked at his mother, then back at the door. His little hand trembled as he turned the knob and opened the door . . . ever so slightly. His mother looked on proudly as her son hearkened to her words, extended his little hand out into the darkness, and yelled loudly, "If you're out there, God, hand me the milk!"

How many people have you known in your life who seemed to be waiting for someone else to hand them the milk? Who let opportunities slip away for fear of failure or rejection? Who lacked the courage at a critical moment to "go for it," to take the risk, to fail, to even succeed? Who were just like you and me? That's right, we have all at one time or another found our courage lacking, and so missed out. We've all at one time or another been that little boy, hoping someone else would hand us the milk and take the risk away.

But risk is what surviving and thriving are all about. And courage, to my way of thinking, is the following:

Courage is the willingness to take a known risk for a known purpose.

Think about it for a moment. Is there anything in life, any skill or quality that you want for yourself or your child, that doesn't require taking a risk? I cannot think of any. Love, honesty, responsibility, cooperation, trust, perseverance—all contain the element of risk, and therefore all require courage to try.

But courage is not blind. Defining it with the phrases "a known risk" for "a known purpose" implies that knowledge is a key element of courage—knowledge that the purpose is worth the risk. Otherwise, we would have to say that the teenager who shoots her body up with drugs on a dare is courageous. But recklessness is not courage. The reckless blind themselves to the real risks and are often unaware of their real purposes. They do this because they actually *lack* the courage to overcome the fear that often comes with risk. The truly courageous are not without fear; they just don't let the fear prevent them from taking risks—knowledgeably and without recklessness.

Discouragement Traps to Avoid

To learn courage, children need the active help of their parents—they need encouragement. But instead, parents often discourage their children in four key ways: (1) by having negative expectations, (2) by focusing on mistakes, (3) by expecting perfection, and (4) by overprotecting. As you read about these discouragement traps, imagine that you are a child, and see how discouraging these traps really are.

Having Negative Expectations

If people who are big and important to you don't believe in your ability, you probably won't believe in it either. They don't have to say so; you can usually tell what they think of you by how they act and what they say. You pick up on those things pretty easily. Of course, sometimes they make their opinions about you very clear by saying things like "You shouldn't do that now, honey; wait until you're bigger," or "While I'm out, you had better not jump on the bed."

CASE 10

On Saturday morning Danny Clarke announced that he was going to prepare his own cereal. "I can do it myself, Mommy," he proudly proclaimed. But his mother reacted anxiously ("No, you're too small; you'll spill it"), so his pride was short-lived. But Danny was adamant, and his mother gave in with a word of caution; "Okay, but be careful and don't spill it." Danny carefully poured the cereal into the bowl, then the milk. The bowl was pretty full as he walked gingerly—almost like a tightrope artist on a high wire—toward the breakfast table. His mother looked on nervously, saying nothing. Finally, Danny reached the table, but as he set the bowl down with a bump, the milk swelled toward the rim and a wave of cereal poured over the edge and onto the table. "See!" scolded his mother. "I told you you'd spill it! Now I have another mess to clean up."

Comment: Children often live up to our expectations—even our negative ones. Danny's mother's negative expectation actually becomes a self-fulfilling prophecy. Her lack of confidence increases her son's anxiety, which in turn increases the tension in his muscles. This tension makes it more difficult to complete a physical task, and, to borrow a sports term, Danny "chokes."

Focusing on Mistakes

If people who are big and important to you spend a lot of time telling you the things you do wrong, you come to believe that there's more wrong with you than right. It gets harder to do right things because you are paying so much attention to your mistakes and blunders. You find yourself losing confidence in your own ability to succeed, and you eventually come to expect failure as the natural outcome. Your own negative expectation then becomes the force that keeps you from improving, from succeeding, and eventually from trying at all.

CASE 11

Jason Bradford's Little League team was not winning many games, although Jason was playing pretty well. His dad, a fine athlete in his day, came to most of the games and joined many of the other bleacher-seat coaches in the stands.

During one particular game, Jason had already made two hits, and his team led by a run in the fourth inning. With two outs and a runner at third—Jason's position—the batter hit a hard ground ball to Jason. Jason had made several plays like this already, but the ball bounced out of his glove and into left field for an error. The runner scored, and Jason's team eventually lost the game.

In the car going home, all his dad could talk about was the error. "Son, you have to concentrate on every play," he reminded Jason. "If you had watched the ball into your glove like we practiced, your team would have kept the lead."

"I know," said Jason dejectedly.

"And another thing," Dr. Bradford said. "When you grounded out your last time at bat, you didn't keep your eye on the ball then either. Did you?"

"I guess not," Jason said lethargically.

"Well, don't let it get you down," said his dad, trying to change the mood. "You'll improve."

Comment: Jason may improve, but if he does, it will be in spite of his father's discouragement, not because of it. By blinding himself to the many positive aspects of his son's game, Dr. Bradford misses a wonderful opportunity to really help. Instead, he harps on the mistakes, discouraging Jason and decreasing his motivation to correct them.

We can certainly learn a lot from our mistakes. But it takes courage for even the most mature of us to tackle mistakes head on. To get this courage, children need to hear a lot more about what they are doing right, rather than wrong. We'll discuss this encouragement technique fully in Chapter 6. Jason's dad can help him correct his mistakes better if he concentrates first on the hits, fine fielding plays, overall effort, and team spirit Jason displayed.

Expecting Perfection

If people who are big and important to you often expect more from you than you are able to give, you begin to feel that you can never satisfy them. If they tell you that you did well, *but* you could have done better, you don't really feel that you did well at all. You begin to wonder if improving is worth the effort. You may stop trying because you believe that you will never satisfy them anyway. You may decide to make your mark in other ways, like misbehaving. You may even set a perfectionistic goal of being the best at being the worst.

CASE 12

Lisa Bradford was on the way to school one morning when her mother stopped her. "Lisa, were you in too big a hurry getting ready this morning?"

"What do you mean?" asked Lisa, on guard.

"Well, your hair doesn't look like it's been brushed very well today."

"Mother! We've been through this before," said Lisa, already exasperated. "My hair is fine the way it is."

" 'Fine' could be 'beautiful' if you'd take a little more time, honey. It's like your dusting. You do it, but you could do it better if you wanted to."

"I guess I just don't want to do it better, then!" snapped Lisa. "Everyone can't be as perfect as you!"

Comment: No matter how hard Lisa tries, she seems to not be living up to somebody's expectation. Her mother sets standards to suit her own perfectionistic style and then tries to impose them on Lisa. Although parents have a responsibility to see that their children do chores correctly and that they meet certain standards of personal hygiene, Lisa's mother shows a lack of tolerance for her daughter's personal style.

The pressure that such perfectionism—the message that nothing is ever good enough—puts on children is tremendously disheartening. Such discouragement usually backfires, and Lisa may stop caring about her appearance and chores at all. Remember how her approach of avoiding schoolwork (discussed in Chapter 4) was the outgrowth of being discouraged over and over again.

Overprotecting

If people who are big and important to you spend a lot of time telling you how dangerous and difficult the world is, you come to believe that you can't handle things for yourself, so you let them do it. If they never let you experience the consequences of mistakes but always bail you out, pretty soon you believe you can do anything you want. But you strangely find yourself not feeling very confident inside (though you may *act* overconfident to make up for it).

CASE 13

Allison Coleman had been in the first grade for several months, and was doing well in all her subjects except one: lunch. No matter how many times her mother reminded Allison to take her lunch, Allison always seemed to forget it at least once a week. Her mother, though annoyed, always brought it to school for her on her way to work.

Comment: You probably realized that Allison is getting contact with her mother through the mistaken approach of seeking undue attention. And her mother makes the situation worse by not allowing Allison to experience the natural consequences of forgetting her lunch (that is, hunger). Her mother is actually overprotecting her. We say *overprotecting* because missing a meal poses no real danger (unless a medical problem exists). Allison has no need of her mom's protection and, in fact, is robbed of an opportunity to learn from her own mistake. Without learning what naturally happens when she forgets her lunch (hunger), Allison learns not only that forgetting lunch is a good way to get undue attention, but also that she can't handle things on her own. Her mother's overprotection fosters this sense of inadequacy, a belief that is eventually very discouraging.

Other Ways Parents Sometimes Misbehave

Parents sometimes misbehave in ways other than falling into the discouragement traps we have just considered. These ways include (1) abuse and neglect, (2) benign neglect, (3) not taking care of the parent, and (4) negative modeling. All of these forms of parental misbehavior can beget misbehavior in children.

Abuse and Neglect

There is a growing awareness of the tragic fact that many parents abuse and/or neglect their children. Abuse usually means either physically hitting a child (other than a spanking, which, though useless, does not qualify as legal abuse), sexually assaulting a child, or psychologically hurting a child through verbal means. Neglect refers to a failure to provide food, clothing, shelter, or adequate protection for a child.

Parents who abuse or neglect their children can be helped through groups such as Parents Anonymous or through counseling. Many of these parents are able to muster the courage to ask for help on their own by calling a community mental health center or Child Protective Services. Others get help when a teacher or doctor or neighbor—anyone who knows what's going on and cares—recognizes his or her responsibility and reports the parent to one of these agencies, or to the police.

Benign Neglect

Benign neglect is a term I use to describe a parent's underinvolvement. Although the child has ample food, clothing, shelter, and protection, he or she lacks something just as important: the parent's contact.

This growing phenomenon is the theme of a movie called *Irreconcilable Differences,* in which an eight-year-old girl "divorces" her parents. Her parents, too busy with their careers, affairs, and infighting, treat her for the most part as if she isn't there. In her touching speech before the court, the little girl asserts that it is wrong to treat a child like the pet you pat on the head when it's convenient.

Unfortunately, too many parents act as if they share the point of view of another character in that movie. When asked at a cocktail party if she has kids, the woman replies, "Oh, yes, I have a kid, but I'm not into parenting right now." Not "into" parenting right now? Has being a parent become a hobby that a person can pick up and drop like tennis? Is being a parent no longer the most important commitment a person can make—a commitment that involves eighteen years of *active* involvement? What has gone wrong?

Perhaps the problem is with us men. For generations we have acted as if what really matters in life occurs outside the home—in the office, at the ballgame, in the trenches. We have often benignly neglected our children, not meaning any harm, just not being there very much or very completely when we are. Fortunately for the children, our wives have covered for us. They have made good on our mutual commitment; they have made the sacrifices; they have been active parents. But we have made it all seem unimportant, not very difficult, and certainly not very satisfying.

Maybe that is why more women have joined their husbands in being "not into parenting right now." But now, with men *and* women shifting their commitment, time, and energy to outside the home, no one is left to cover the home base. Our children are sometimes benignly neglected.

What's the answer? For women to work only within the home for eighteen years? For men to take a turn in the home for the next millennium? Not practical on either count. And what about child care—isn't there a place for it? I think so, but the place of child care is not to replace the parents. It can't do that adequately.

I think the solution is twofold. First, we have to reestablish our priorities. Parenting children is the most important job we have, and it is also the most human and therefore the most potentially satisfying. Second, we need to go ahead and involve ourselves outside the home *in moderation.* We need to avoid being overwhelmed trying to "be all that you can be." Regardless of what Madison Avenue wants us to believe, we can*not* have it all! We need to let some opportunities get away from us. We don't have to set the world on fire. We can play the game out there in moderation, knowing full well that the really *big* game is at home with our families.

Not Taking Care of the Parent

Being an active parent, as you well know, takes a tremendous amount of energy. When we are tired, when we haven't slept well, when we haven't gotten the proper nourishment, we lose energy rapidly. When that happens, we often become irritable and quarrelsome, and we're more likely to engage in power struggles and behave discouragingly.

Part of being a parent is taking care of the parent. This not only means maintaining good eating, sleeping, and exercising habits, but also taking time away from your children. As I stressed in the section on benign neglect, such time is better taken in moderation, but moderation works both ways. If you are with your children almost all of the time, then you probably are not taking good enough care of yourself to be the parent you would like to be. Usually, the younger your child, the more time and energy he or she requires. But it is important, even with infants, for you to take some time for exercise and recreation (as well as rest!). Getting your spouse to help out is a good place to start. Relatives (especially grandparents) can be a tremendous resource. Swapping child care with a neighbor or even hiring someone to babysit for brief periods can be effective.

Also remember that your marriage requires time and energy. When parents neglect their partners, the tension that ensues is destructive to everyone in the family. Again, balance and moderation are the key. If you are a single parent, then a social life requires this same balance of time and energy.

Negative Modeling

Social learning theory has established quite clearly what grandparents have always known: "Children learn what they live." Setting an example through our actions is called modeling. As we model our values and beliefs through our behavior, our children watch, listen, and learn. In fact, they pay a great deal more attention to what we do than to what we say. Consequently, if we want them to learn useful qualities and values, we must first live (and model) such values. The old admonition to "do as I say, not as I do" just doesn't work.

Whenever we create a discrepancy between what we say we value and how we behave, we both erode our credibility and provide a negative model. For example:

DO YOU SAY YOU VALUE?	BUT DO YOU ALSO?
Honesty	Lie to friends ("Tell her I'm not home")?
Fairness	Always demand what you want ("Let's go see this movie; you'll like it too")?
Education	Watch TV all evening every night?
Respect	Call your child names or insult him or her ("You're so clumsy I don't believe it")?
Health	Smoke, overeat, or fail to exercise?
Responsibility	Blame others when things go wrong?
Forgiveness	Feel guilty reading this chart?

Forgiveness and Change Versus Guilt

You've probably had a hard time reading this chapter. Being a parent involves so many pitfalls that getting to this point in the book without recognizing at least some of the mistakes you have made is virtually impossible. If you have hung in this far, please give yourself a big pat on the back for having shown, in Dreikurs's words, the courage to be imperfect.

At this point, you have a choice. You can forgive yourself for your imperfections and correct your mistakes, or you can punish yourself with guilt and continue the mistaken behavior. Believe it or not, it is forgiveness rather than guilt that paves the way for change. Guilt is just the price we pay to continue misbehaving.

In Part II, you will see how to turn the pitfalls of discouragement into opportunities for encouragement. Why not leave any guilt you're experiencing right here, and begin focusing on what you are already doing well? As you read Part II, you will recognize many of your own strengths as a parent. Correcting mistakes and building on strengths is the best way to pursue excellence in anything—including being a parent.

The Methods of Active Parenting

6

Instilling Courage: The Power of Encouragement

Children need encouragement like plants need water.

RUDOLF DREIKURS

Preparing a child to meet courageously the challenges that life will certainly offer is perhaps the single most important aspect of being an active parent. Courage is such an important quality in today's complex world of choices that we have said that it forms the foundation upon which the child constructs his or her personality. From the French word *coeur* for heart, courage is the heart that enables us to develop responsibility, cooperativeness, the ability to love—and whatever other qualities we may strive for.

The previous chapter described how you can begin to cut down on your behaviors that dis-courage your child. This chapter will help you begin the process of actually instilling courage—of en-couragement.

What Is Encouragement?

Imagine yourself in this situation: You are driving your car home from work or from shopping. Suddenly, in your rearview mirror you see a police car following you, its blue lights flashing. Anxiously, you pull over, wondering what you did wrong. You notice your rapid heartbeat, the perspiration forming on your palms, your dry mouth. The police officer approaches your car window and asks for your driver's license. She looks at the license, then at you, and says, "You know, I've been on the force for twelve years, and it's always a pleasure to see a courteous driver. I pulled you over so I could congratulate you on the fine driving skill you showed back there in that traffic tangle at the freeway overpass. If every driver were as courteous and considerate as you, we would avoid a lot of snarls and headaches. So I just wanted to say thanks."

How do you think you would react to the police officer's comment?

A. You would feel good about yourself; you'd be a little proud.

B. You would feel that you are a pretty good driver.

C. You would feel encouraged to drive more courteously and considerately in the future.

D. You'd almost faint from the shock!

D would probably be your strongest response. We just do not expect to receive such compliments from authority figures. We have been systematically taught to expect the worst—from teachers, from police officers, from our own parents. And yet, after the shock had worn off and you were driving away, you probably would feel good about yourself, think you were a pretty good driver, and feel encouraged to drive more courteously and considerately in the future.

This imaginary situation is an example of the power of encouragement. Only a few words can increase your self-esteem, give your confidence a boost, and create the likelihood that you will drive even better in the future. No wonder we call encouragement the subtle giant.

In fact, encouragement is the most powerful form of influence that psychologists have yet to discover. When used skillfully and systematically, it can produce tremendous change. Parents who want their children to thrive can use encouragement to (1) provide a base of courage *and* (2) influence their children to move in positive directions. (A word of caution, however, is also in order. Like any powerful tool, encouragement can be used for negative purposes as well as positive ones. Fanatics, for instance, have gone so far as to *encourage* acts of terrorism and even suicide.)

Encouragement Methods to Use

We have already looked at four common ways that parents discourage their children. Let's now see how each of these ways can be flip-flopped into methods to encourage.

HOW TO DISCOURAGE	HOW TO ENCOURAGE
1. Have negative expectations.	**1.** Show confidence.
2. Focus on mistakes.	**2.** Build on strengths.
3. Expect perfection.	**3.** Value the child.
4. Give too much protection.	**4.** Stimulate independence.

In the next few pages we're going to concentrate on these four key ways in which you, as a parent, can encourage your child.

Showing Confidence

Your confidence in your child's ability is a bedrock, a base of security, from which he or she can reach upward and outward. With your confidence as support, your child can discover that he or she has talents and abilities and strengths. Some ways you can demonstrate your confidence are by giving your child responsibility, asking your child's opinion, and avoiding the temptation to rescue your child.

Give responsibility. Giving a child responsibility is a way of expressing confidence, of saying, "I know that you can do this." Of course, you need to give responsibility in line with what you know your child's abilities to be, or else you may set your child up for failure. Here are some examples of ways to demonstrate confidence:

- "You may keep the dog, Julie, if you will accept the responsibility for feeding and caring for her."

- "I think you have handled getting yourself up in the morning really well, and so you can probably handle staying up later now—say until 10:00 P.M. What do you think?"

Ask your child's opinion or advice. Older children, especially teenagers, like to have parents lean on their knowledge or judgment. If you ask their advice, you are saying that you have confidence in their opinion. If you ask them to teach you to do things they know how to do, you are saying that you have confidence in their skills and knowledge. Asking for their input bolsters their feelings of self-worth:

- "Which route do you think would be best on our trip across the country?"

- "What would you like to do with the toys that got left on the floor?"

- "Would you teach me how to use the new computer?"

- "Well, what *were* the purposes of the Civil War?"

Avoid the temptation to rescue. Most of all, you show confidence in your child's abilities when you refuse to step in and take over when he or she is discouraged. What a temptation it is, this tendency to do what is so hard for them and so easy for you! But if you give in to the temptation, you are demonstrating that you don't have confidence in his or her ability to follow a task or a project through to the end, even when the going gets rough. Rescuing doesn't encourage children who are discouraged; it certifies their discouragement. Such children often become unable to tolerate frustration, and when things don't work out immediately, they often have frustration tantrums. Encourage rather than rescue:

- "Keep trying; you can do it!"

- "Attaboy! Just a little more and you'll have it."

CASE 10 (UPDATE)

Danny's mother recognized that her own negative expectations had not only been discouraging, but had actually contributed to her son's spilling his cereal. Rather than feeling guilty about her mistake, she just chalked it up to the learning process and began looking for opportunities to show confidence in Danny. She was surprised at how many there were.

"Danny, will you help me make the pancakes by mixing this? You do such a good job."

"Which pajamas would you like to wear tonight, the blue ones or the ones from planet Zork?"

She even waited for him to give the cereal another try, but he steadfastly avoided carrying another bowl. After about a week, she poured the milk into the cereal and left it on the counter. "Danny," she said, "I think you can handle carrying the cereal over to the table without spilling any. How about it?"

Danny's eyes lit up at her confidence, but then a wave of fear swept across his face as he remembered last time. "You can do it," encouraged his mother. And as he lifted the bowl and began his walk, she added, "That's it, just a little more." Danny carefully put the bowl on the table, but a little bit of cereal still managed to defy gravity and spill over the side of the bowl. "That's okay," said Danny's mother. "You did a really good job. Here's a sponge." As Danny cleaned up the spilled milk, she added, "You know, next time I bet you won't spill any at all."

Building on Strengths

Another way of encouraging children is to concentrate on what's right with them, instead of what's wrong. You can build more easily on your child's strengths than on his or her mistakes. When you point out your child's strong points, he or she is more likely to show you that trait again, and soon. Some ways to build on strengths are to acknowledge what your child does well, to give credit for strengths even when your child uses them inappropriately, to concentrate on improvement rather than perfection, to give positive strokes with each step, and to avoid labeling your child's personality.

Acknowledge what your child does well. It's much more effective to "catch 'em being good" than to catch children being bad. With only a little effort, you can notice and comment on the many things your child does well. Just a few occasional words can work wonders. Along the same lines, you can express appreciation for help with tasks, even those that are assigned as your child's share of family duties. Don't take your child's efforts for granted; try using phrases like the following and watch his or her efforts redouble:

- "It was really a pleasure having you out to dinner with us tonight. Your manners were great. Let's do it again soon."

- "Thank you for helping me with the dishes."

- "I appreciate the way you played quietly while I took a nap. That was very considerate."

- "I like the way you shared your orange with Bernice."

- "You sure helped with the garden."

■ "It sure is fun to play with you when you take turns with me."

Give credit for strengths, even when used inappropriately. We can encourage children even when they repeatedly misbehave. Focusing on a child's strengths in these cases makes it easier to like the child. And when you focus on what you like, the child often gets better. For example, if a child is rebellious, you can say, "I know you don't often do what I ask you, and that's pretty frustrating for me. But I have to admit, I really admire your courage in standing up for yourself."

Concentrate on improvement, not perfection. Children get a sense of worth from attaining excellence in something—a sport, a school subject, or a skill. Excellence, however, requires many steps and much improvement. Your encouragement is more valuable along the way than it is after your child has already reached excellence. Your encouragement is also most valuable when it is directed toward the efforts your child makes, regardless of whether those efforts succeed or fail.

■ "You are really improving in your reading. I can hear the difference."

■ "You really gave it a good try."

■ "I can see the effort that went into this."

Give positive strokes with each step. When you're teaching your child a new skill or behavior, tell your child what he or she is already doing well. If you break the new skill down into its smallest steps, the child can experience success with each one, and you can comment on each success. In this way, you encourage your child to try each new step with confidence, and he or she can learn even difficult tasks. Also, keep in mind that one "attaboy" or "attagirl" is better than a dozen bullwhips!

■ "You did a good job pulling the sheets and blankets up. Would you like some help tucking them in?"

■ "That's it; you've got the laces crossed. Now let's try pulling this one under—Good!"

■ "Attaboy! Keep it up. This room is really starting to look good."

Giving positive strokes with each step can also help to change your child's bad habits. For example, if you want to teach your son to stop hitting his little sister, decide to look for *any* improvement in his behavior toward her; then encourage it. You may have to look hard. Maybe you can catch him *not* hitting her. If so, you might say when you're alone with him, "I noticed that you didn't hit your sister a single time during the show; thanks, sweety." Then give him a kiss. Or maybe you can catch him actually helping her. "Hey, I like the way you're teaching your sister to put the pegs in the hole. You're good at it."

Avoid labeling a child's personality. By connecting any positive movement in the right direction with a word of encouragement, you increase the chances that your chld will do more of the same. But be aware that what you think is encouraging may come across to your child as *discouraging.* Praise such as "You're such a *good* boy" often has this discouraging effect. A child often sees the flip side of the praise and wonders how long it will be before he is labeled a *bad* boy. Labeling a child's personality, even with a positive label, can therefore discourage. Because children (as well as adults) have much more control over their behavior than their basic personalities, it is more encouraging to focus our judgment on children's actions. Each child is different, so get to know what *your* child experiences as encouraging.

CASE 11 (UPDATE)

Once he had a clear look at how he was focusing on his son's errors at third base, Jason's dad had an opportunity to begin building on strengths. It worked so well that by basketball season, Jason was actually seeking out his help.

One Saturday, while he and Jason were playing a game of H-O-R-S-E, Dr. Bradford made a reverse lay-up that he hadn't tried in years. Jason was impressed, and after the game asked his dad to show him how to do it.

Dr. Bradford took it step by step so that he would have plenty of chances to encourage Jason along the way. "Okay, Jason, the first thing is to get your steps right. You want to come out from under the backboard on your left foot. Let's try it from here and just take three steps. Watch me. Okay, left . . . right . . . left and up. Now you try it, and don't worry about whether the ball goes in, just concentrate on the steps."

The first step wasn't too difficult for Jason, and it gave his father a chance to add, "Attaboy, you got it. Now, let's move back a little and add the dribble."

So it went, with Dr. Bradford encouraging his son with each bit of improvement. Whenever Jason missed, Dr. Bradford showed his confidence: "No problem. You can do it. Try again." Before long, Jason had mastered the reverse lay-up, and more important, increased his courage.

Valuing the Child

Children's self-worth does not spring from achievements alone. It comes much more from being accepted regardless of whether they behave or misbehave, succeed or fail. The message that your child is good enough right now, just as he or she is, conveys a large dose of encouragement. You can deliver this message by separating your child's worth from accomplishments and mistakes, and by appreciating your child's uniqueness.

Separate worth from accomplishments. A child's worth does not depend on what the child *does*, but on who he or she *is*. You can admire your child's accomplishments, but make it clear that you love your child for himself or herself. Put your emphasis on supporting your child's activities, not just on praising the results of those activities. Encourage your child *while* he or she is doing something instead of after the task is completed. And *de*-emphasize competition, since research clearly indicates that cooperation is more productive. The appropriate person for the child to compete with is himself or herself; self-improvement, rather than winning, is the goal. Some examples:

- "I'm glad you enjoy learning."
- "It's nice to get good grades, especially when you've put so much effort into it."
- "You look like you're really into this report."
- "It's more important to play your best than to win."
- "Losing doesn't make a person a loser."
- "We love *you*, not your grades."
- "It's fun to play for the fun of it."

Separate worth from mistakes. Just as your child's worth is something different from his or her accomplishments, so is it different from his or her mistakes and failures. There are no bad children, only bad behavior. Children who are labeled bad often enough come to think of themselves as bad, and bad behavior then seems appropriate to them. For this reason, it is important for parents to correct children who label themselves as bad.

Mistakes, like bad behavior, do not indicate lack of worth, but are actually a part of growth and development. A mistake can show a child what not to do in the future, which is certainly a valuable lesson. Children and adults who are afraid of imperfection actually retard their own self-improvement and excellence.

Do you know what a perfectionist is? A person who won't study a foreign language until he can already speak it fluently. As this quip implies, a fear of mistakes yields a fear of trying, which in turn yields less learning. Since our goal is to help children learn, we have to help them make friends with mistakes. Here are some ways:

- "No, *you're* not bad, but it *is* bad to crayon on the walls."
- "When we get angry at you, it doesn't mean we don't like you. It means we don't like something you've done."
- "Walls are not for finger painting. Paper is for finger painting."
- "Mistakes are for learning. When we make a mistake, we don't blame. We correct it."
- "I guess you made a mistake. Well, let's see what you can learn from it."

Appreciate your child's uniqueness. Although it is important to treat children as equals, that doesn't mean that children are all the same. Children are encouraged when they feel that they are unique, special, and one of a kind. You can appreciate your child's uniqueness by taking an interest in his or her activities. Your interest can encourage your child by validating his or her experience as interesting and worthwhile, as long as you avoid passing judgments or engaging in investigative questioning. Most of all, you can say and do things that show that you love your child for his or her unique self and not for any other reason. Here are some of these things you can say:

- "You really look good in yellow."
- "Anyway, that's my opinion. What's *yours?*"
- "When I see you from a distance, I can tell it's you from your walk."
- "You are the only you in the whole world. What luck that you happen to be my daughter!"
- "You're a neat kid, you know it?"
- "I like you."
- "I love you."

CASE 12 (UPDATE)

The Bradfords eventually came to understand that their perfectionism was getting in the way of their relationship with Lisa and was discouraging her efforts to improve. They both agreed that since Lisa was their child, and for no other reason, she was special to them and of unparalleled value. They decided to look for ways to communicate that they did value *her*, and not just her accomplishments.

Her dad found a wonderful opportunity to express his valuing Lisa while she was putting herself down for a mediocre biology grade. After talking with Lisa about her plans for improving, he looked her in the eye, touched her shoulder, and said, "I'll tell you this, though, I wouldn't trade you for all the A's on all the biology tests in the world."

Lisa's mom shared a similar story. By focusing on Lisa's real importance to her, she had actually become more aware that she really did value Lisa. One afternoon she told Lisa that she had been looking through a family photo album that morning and had come across an old picture of Lisa at about four years old, playing in a small plastic swimming pool. "You were having such a good time," she recalled, "that I could almost hear that good-hearted laugh of yours coming right out of the photo. Then I thought to myself how much I would have missed had I never heard that laugh." Both Lisa's and her mother's eyes welled with tears as they hugged each other.

Stimulating Independence

Independence is standing on your own two feet, without leaning on another. Since that is what every child must learn to do in order to become a functioning adult, cultivating independence is an essential aspect of child development. At the same time, enormous benefits can be derived from cooperation. "No man is an island" expresses the truth that interdependence is essential for the development of the human species. You can offer encouragement by stimulating your child to rely on his or her own abilities and, at the same time, to contribute those abilities cooperatively to working, playing, and associating with others.

Let your child do things for himself or herself. It is in learning to do things on their own that children overcome feelings of being little or helpless. Gradually, and step by step, children master their environment, gaining confidence and increasing feelings of self-worth in the process. You can help by letting your child first do things he or she can do and then learn from the natural consequences of those actions when possible. It is discouraging for a parent to do for a child on a regular basis what the child can do for herself or himself. Gently encourage your child to conquer fears. Let your child set the pace; don't push, but do offer support for each venture.

Take time for training. As your child learns to do the little things, such as washing and getting dressed, he or she becomes more independent. The time you spend teaching your child how to do these things is time well spent for both of you. Independence is also stimulated when a child learns to make decisions. For practice in decision making, give your child choices to make. Here are some examples of things to say that stimulate independence:

- "How would you like your eggs, hard or soft?"

- "You can handle it."

- "You're getting able to take care of yourself."

- "You can put your shirt on by yourself now."

- "You want us to think you can't do it, but we think you can."

- "Do you want to try swimming to me from the other side of the pool? I'll be here if you have any trouble."

- "Here, let me show you how to do it."

- "Do you want to practice pouring?"

- "Would you rather have orange or apple juice this morning?"

- "How would you like to handle it?"

Help your child develop a sense of interdependence. Because belonging is the basic social need in human beings, it deserves special emphasis. Invite cooperative behavior on the part of your child, with the aim of letting him or her experience the pleasure and benefit of group efforts. Here are some ways:

- "You're a part of this family, and we'd like your input at family council."

- "We're all in it together."

- "Would you like some help in organizing your room?"

- "Would you like to make cookies with us?"

- "You come too."

CASE 13 (UPDATE)

Allison's mother thought that she was being a "good parent" by bringing Allison's lunch to school whenever she forgot it. When I explained to her that she was really overprotecting Allison and that the underlying discouragement actually triggered other problems, her mother was ready to try a new approach to lunch.

I encouraged Allison's mother to accept the responsibility for the overprotection herself, rather than blaming Allison. She did this beautifully, and said, "Allison, I've been thinking about all those times that I've brought your lunch to school for you. I want to apologize for treating you like a baby, like you couldn't handle lunch on your own. From now on, I'm going to mind my own business and leave your lunch in your lunchbox for you to remember. Should I leave it on the table or on the counter?"

The next time Allison called from school, her mother told her, "Gee, honey, I'm sorry you forgot your lunch, but I know you can handle it on your own."

"Can't *you* bring it to me?" pleaded Allison.

"That would be treating you like a baby, remember? I don't want to do that anymore, but you can have your afternoon snack when you get home, and we'll have a good dinner tonight. I love you, sweetheart. Bye."

Letter of Encouragement

As a young Sunday school teacher, I became annoyed with the idea of having to give grades to my students. Grades seemed an inadequate way to express either their progress or the way that I felt about them after we had shared nine months together. So I decided to write each student a personal letter to go with his or her grade. While writing the letters, I found myself describing only the positive aspects of each child and how he or she was progressing. The children received these "letters of encouragement" appreciatively as they left for summer vacation.

I didn't think much more about the letters until four years later. I was at a reception when a woman approached me, introducing herself as the mother of one of my students from that same Sunday school class. "That letter you wrote Alice," she said, "meant so much to her, and you know, she still has it on her bulletin board."

All of the encouragement skills discussed in this chapter are important and should become part of your child's daily diet. But from time to time it's very useful to put them to work in a letter of encouragement. Somehow putting it in writing carries extra weight in our society. In addition, the child can refer back to a letter of encouragement in the future and rekindle the warm feeling that it generated, just as Alice did. As you write to your child, keep in mind the following points:

- Write about improvement in some area, not necessarily perfection.

- Write only truthful statements; don't say your child has improved when he or she really hasn't.

- Be specific about what the improvements have been.

- Say how your child's behavior has been helpful to others. *For example:*

DEAR JOHNNY,

Your father and I were working in the garden and we noticed that you had already started weeding around the tomatoes. Both of us are so pleased that you are helping us! The garden is a big job and your participation really counts. It won't be long before we can all enjoy our first salad—a gift from the garden. We are looking forward to it.

Thanks,
MOM AND DAD

ACTION PAGE 4

Practice using encouraging statements this week. Choose one specific day to encourage each child. For example, on Tuesday, concentrate on encouraging David, on Wednesday, encourage Melody, and so on. Using the following chart, make a check mark each time you make an encouraging statement.

CHILD'S NAME	DAY	CHECK OFF EACH ENCOURAGING STATEMENT

7

Strengthening
Relationships

*Respect is what you have to have in
order to get.*

BERNARD MALAMUD

By this time, you may be chomping at the bit for some solid discipline
techniques. "I don't want to hear any more about being positive," you
may be saying. "My child won't behave and I've run out of patience.
You told me back in Chapter 2 that punishment doesn't work well
anymore. So tell me already, *how do I discipline my child?!*"

Well, we are almost there. But remember, discipline, as important
as it is, does not occur in a vacuum. It always occurs within the context
of the relationship between you and your child. When that relationship
is a good one, discipline—enforcing limits—is easy. On the other hand,
when your relationship has deteriorated into a power struggle or revenge match, discipline is very difficult and often makes matters even
worse. A child who hears only "no" or "don't" becomes discouraged.
And discouragement, as we know, leads to further misbehavior.

For this reason, half of the job of disciplining your child is to first develop a strong positive relationship. The encouragement methods described in Chapter 6 are an excellent way to begin this process. In this chapter, we will focus on four specific methods for strengthening your relationship with your child: (1) taking time for fun, (2) teaching your child skills, (3) building mutual respect, and (4) expressing love. Each can be done regularly—some every day—and each, of course, should be done with encouragement.

Taking Time for Fun

Having fun is a common way for relationships to begin and to grow. When you share a happy experience with your child, each of you subconsciously associates that pleasurable feeling with the other, and your relationship is strengthened.

Unfortunately, as parents become busier and busier, they often find less and less time for having fun with their children. They use their limited time to take care of what they view as more essential tasks of being a parent: cleaning, cooking, shopping, and discipline. By the time these tasks are finished, little time or energy is left for having fun.

I think this is a mistake. These other tasks are important, but I would rather see a child eat a peanut butter and jelly sandwich for dinner if it meant that he or she could have ten minutes that day playing "death by tickling" with his mom or dad.

Making it a point to spend at least ten minutes a day doing something fun with each of your children will pay rich dividends to both of you. Fun time can be a one-to-one experience or it can be something that several of you can enjoy together. Some examples of fun activities:

- Read a story
- Play catch
- Do a puzzle
- Sing a song
- Make popcorn
- Roughhouse

A few tips may help you get the most out of this activity:

- Find activities that you both enjoy.

- Ask for suggestions from your child, and be ready to offer suggestions.

- Keep it fun! Do not use this time for confronting or trying to handle problems.

- Record your experience in a notebook or journal, or on the chart on the following page.

CHILD'S NAME	WHAT DID YOU DO?	HOW DID IT GO?
SUN.		
MON.		
TUES.		
_____ WED.		
THUR.		
FRI.		
SAT.		
SUN.		
MON.		
TUES.		
_____ WED.		
THUR.		
FRI.		
SAT.		

CASE 14

Danny Clarke wanted to watch a scary movie on TV one Friday night. His mother remembered that the last time he had watched a horror movie, he had had nightmares all night long. She did not want a repeat performance of the episode, but did not want to discourage him, either. She decided to take the opportunity to create some fun for the two of them.

"Please, Mommy. I want to see the monster," pleaded Danny.

"Okay, Danny, but we don't need those silly TV monsters. I've got a *real* monster in my closet," replied his mom.

Danny giggled, "You don't have a *real* monster, Mommy."

"Oh, but I do," she said. "You wait right here for five minutes, and you'll see for yourself. Are you brave enough?"

"Let me see," said Danny excitedly.

"Okay, the monster is afraid of light, so here's the deal. Let's set the timer for five minutes, and when the buzzer on the timer sounds, you have to turn off the lights so he'll come out, okay? You can use this," she said, handing Danny a flashlight. "If he gives you any trouble, just shine the light in his eyes. Be sure to wait right here."

She hurried to the bedroom and quickly covered her face with white powder and awful lipstick. She then wrapped a sheet around herself, and when the buzzer sounded and Danny turned out the lights, she put her flashlight under her chin so that it shined on her face, and entered the living room.

"I—am—the—ghost—of—Hackensack," said Danny's mother, who had never even lived in New Jersey. "And—I—eat—little—boys—named—Danny!"

As she walked ominously toward her prey, Danny shined his light in her eyes, and said, "Take that, you ghost of Have-a-sack!"

"No, not light!" squealed the monster, recoiling. "I look so awful in the light."

As Danny came closer with the light, his mom grabbed him and proceeded to "eat" his stomach, which caused a lot of laughing on both sides as they rolled around the living room. Later, they made a monster costume for Danny, and he played the ghost of Peoria, though he had never lived in Illinois.

ACTION PAGE 5

Recall something fun that you enjoyed doing as a child with one of your parents. Close your eyes for a moment and visualize the experience.

1. WHAT WAS THE ACTIVITY THAT YOU AND YOUR PARENT SHARED?

2. HOW DID YOU FEEL ABOUT YOUR PARENT AT THAT MOMENT?

3. HOW DID YOU FEEL ABOUT YOURSELF?

Teaching Your Child Skills

In Chapter 3 we saw how belonging, learning, and contributing lead to self-esteem. Teaching a skill to a child touches on all three. The contact between you and your child supports a sense of belonging. The skill itself is learned, thereby fostering power. Finally, having learned something new, the child now has something else to contribute to others.

As a parent, if you generate such self-esteem in your child, you will certainly strengthen your relationship with her or him. In addition, by empowering your child with knowledge, you give him or her a positive way to approach the basic goal of power, which is particularly valuable for a child who is pursuing power via the mistaken approach of rebellion. Teaching useful skills offers an excellent means of helping your child get or stay on the right track.

The following steps will help you be an effective teacher as you empower your child:

1. *Motivate.* Encourage your child to want to learn by explaining the value the skill has to the child and to the entire family. For example, say, "The family needs your help in folding clothes."
2. *Select a good time.* Pick a time when you won't feel rushed and when neither you nor your child are upset about other things.

3. *Demonstrate.* Show your child how to perform the skill, explaining slowly as you do. For example, say, "The corners of the washcloths need to be even, like this."

4. *Let your child try.* Let your child perform the skill while you watch, ready to help if he or she cannot complete it. It may take several tries. Be gentle, not critical about mistakes. Let it be fun.

5. *Work together.* Once your child has learned the skill in question, work along with him or her for a time, so that you both can enjoy the companionship of labor. It can be a delightful experience for you both.

6. *Acknowledge efforts.* Make comments concerning your child's efforts and progress. For example, say, "You worked really hard folding the washcloths. Thanks."

Here are a few tips to help the teaching-learning process flow smoothly:

- Accept your child's efforts for what they are. The corners may not be as square as you would like them to be, but who is hurt?

- Provide some choices. For example, say, "Would you like to fold towels or washcloths?"

- Be patient. Learning new skills takes time.

- Make it fun. Turn on the radio, or sing, or make it a game.

- Be on guard for signs of discouragement. Encourage often.

- Again, it is helpful to record your experiences in a journal or notebook.

ACTION PAGE 6

Recall a skill that one of your parents taught you. Again, close your eyes for a moment and visualize the learning experience.

1. WHAT WAS THE ACTIVITY?

2. HOW DID YOU FEEL ABOUT YOUR PARENT AT THAT MOMENT?

3. HOW DID YOU FEEL ABOUT YOURSELF?

4. WHAT CAN YOU LEARN FROM THE MEMORY?

Mistakes to avoid:

Things to do:

ACTION PAGE 6 (continued)

Now you try. Pick an activity you would like to work on with your child this week. Possible activities are:

- Putting toys away
- Folding clothes
- Making beds
- Dressing self
- Setting the table
- Swimming

- Riding a bike
- Cooking
- Sports
- Building
- Repairs
- Driving

List the names of your children and what skill you have decided to teach each child.

CHILD'S NAME	SKILL TO BE TAUGHT
1.	
2.	
3.	

After you teach the skill, use the six steps as a checklist:

1. Did you *motivate* the child?

2. Did you *select a good time* when you weren't rushed?

3. Did you *demonstrate* how to do this job?

4. Did you *let him or her try*?

5. Did you *work alongside* your child?

6. Did you *acknowledge his or her efforts?*

WHAT WENT WELL WITH EACH CHILD?

WHAT MIGHT YOU DO TO IMPROVE THE EXPERIENCE NEXT TIME?

CASE 15

Although Lisa was still having difficulty with schoolwork, her mother realized that she was not very good at tutoring her daughter and that her attempts to do so usually left them both feeling discouraged. She felt a great sense of relief when I suggested that a parent is seldom the best person to help with schoolwork. Teachers, tutors, and class-mates are much better equipped to provide extra help. Parents can do more good by teaching other skills. What was she good at, I asked, that Lisa might want to learn?

"That's easy," said her mom. "Lisa just turned fifteen and is dying to learn how to drive."

So, armed with a learner's permit and the family car, Lisa and her mom headed out to a large shopping center parking lot on Sunday afternoon. Motivation was no problem, and Sunday was a good time for both of them. On the way, Lisa's mom demonstrated—in slow motion—the steps involved in starting a car, checking the mirrors, and fastening the seat belts. She also explained where she looked and what she was doing as they drove down the street.

Once at the deserted lot, she encouraged Lisa to try: "Okay, now it's your turn." Lisa was both excited and nervous as she got behind the wheel.

"Okay, honey, you're going to do fine; I can feel it. Now, what's the first thing you check when you get behind the wheel?"

"The tape deck?" giggled Lisa, as she adjusted the rearview mirror.

Building Mutual Respect

Respect is a highly important aspect of all relationships in a democratic society; its absence erodes the possibility of cooperation and breeds resentment and hostility. Teaching children respect is, therefore, an important goal for the active parent.

How do we teach this basic skill? All parents want their children to show them respect. But as the Malamud quote suggests, "Respect is what you have to have in order to get." Dreikurs's concept of mutual respect between parent and child is an idea that many parents have found invaluable: the best way to teach respect is to show it.

Most adults have learned how to show respect toward other adults; yet, parents so easily slip into disrespect when addressing their own children. We humiliate; we criticize; we nag, belittle, remind, yell, label, name-call, and intimidate; we do for children what they could do for themselves; we put ourselves in their service; we allow them to abuse us; we don't listen when they talk; and we become furious when they return in kind. The list goes on and on.

Why do we treat our children disrespectfully, and how can we catch ourselves first? The answer to the first question is that disrespect has probably become part of the traditional way of being a parent handed down to us through our own parents. To check this out, think about your own parents as you complete the following activity.

CASE 16

Dexter Coleman's mother shared a particularly illuminating dream.

"You know how I sometimes get on Dex's case about his chores? Well, I guess after a hard day's work, I get a little carried away at times and yell at him. Yesterday, for instance, he was listening to some rock and roll on his headphones when I reminded him that the dishes needed washing. He didn't move fast enough, because I sort of lost it—ran into the living room, yanked his earphones off, and told him to move when I say move!

"That night I had this weird dream. I was lying on the couch listening to a Brahms symphony, when Dex asked me to iron a shirt for him. I guess I didn't move fast enough, because before I knew it, he had yanked my headphones off and was shouting at me to 'move when I say move!' It was like he was the parent—like my father used to yell at me. I swore I'd never treat a child of mine like that, but I guess I have.

"The next morning I told Dex about my dream and apologized to him for the disrespect I had shown. He felt really good about it. I did, too, and I've been a lot more respectful since then."

Expressing Love

Building a positive relationship with your child is an ongoing process, and it takes steady effort. As we have seen, it involves making arrangements to have fun together, teaching specific skills, and building mutual respect. But the positive relationship between parent and child involves, most of all, expressing love for each other. All children hunger for love, even those who make a career of being unlovable. Children need to know that, whatever else may happen, their parents love them.

Your own method of expressing your love to your child can be woven into the fabric of everyday life: a kiss, a pat on the back, a tousling of hair, an arm around the shoulder. But it is equally important to be able to say to your child that you love him or her. The words may come awkwardly for you; they do for some parents. But the important thing is how beautiful they sound to a child!

You can say "I love you" at an unexpected time, when your child will be surprised at the timing, but pleased with the message. You can say "I love you" at a time of calmness or tenderness, such as bedtime, and your child can bask in the warmth of the words. You can even say "I love you" as a nonsensical answer to a child's question, if you want to get the message across without being too serious about it:

"Daddy, why are you hammering on the wall?"

"Because I love you."

"Oh, that's not why."

"Maybe not, but I do."

CASE 17

Jason and his dad had had their ups and downs, but through encouragement and more respectful discipline methods, things had improved greatly. They were having fun together more often. Dr. Bradford had taught his son many skills—from basketball to his famous Belgian waffle technique.

But one thing was particularly difficult for him—saying "I love you." Having grown up in a family that didn't express much affection, he just couldn't get the words out. He thought about it often, but somehow he always felt foolish when an opportunity arose, and he clammed up.

Finally, almost by accident, it happened. He and Jason had been passing a football back and forth in the yard. Jason pretended to intercept a pass, and ran toward his dad. Although they didn't touch much (again, he felt funny), Dr. Bradford came up and playfully tackled Jason. He pulled the ball away and began to run, but Jason grabbed his leg. The two of them began rolling around the yard, laughing as they rolled over and over each other. The ball lay off to the side as they playfully wrestled. Finally, exhausted, they lay on the ground with Dr. Bradford holding his son from behind in a bear hug.

"Say 'uncle'?" he said.

"Why should I say 'uncle'?" laughed Jason. "You're not my uncle; you're my dad."

"You're right," he said. "And you're my son, and I love you."

Dr. Bradford wasn't sure what it was, but something seemed to happen when he said those words. A barrier had been broken, and he felt a strong bond created in its place.

ACTION PAGE 7

A. Almost every child is treated disrespectfully by his or her parents at times. Remembering when we felt disrespected as children can help us learn how to treat our own children respectfully.

1. WHAT WERE SOME WAYS THAT YOUR FATHER WAS DISRESPECTFUL OF YOU?

2. HOW DID YOU FEEL ABOUT HIM AT SUCH TIMES?

Did you feel respect for him?   **Yes   No**

Did you feel cooperative?   **Yes   No**

3. WHAT WERE SOME WAYS THAT YOUR MOTHER WAS DISRESPECTFUL OF YOU?

4. HOW DID YOU FEEL ABOUT HER AT SUCH TIMES?

Did you feel respect for her?   **Yes   No**

Did you feel cooperative?   **Yes   No**

5. WHAT ARE SOME WAYS THAT YOU HAVE BEEN DISRESPECTFUL OF YOUR CHILDREN?

ACTION PAGE 7 (continued)

B. To catch yourself before you behave in a disrespectful way, each time you interact with your child this week, imagine that he or she is an adult. Speak with the same respect you would use with another adult.

At the end of the week, answer the following questions:

1. WHAT CHANGES DID YOU NOTE IN YOUR OWN BEHAVIOR WITH YOUR CHILD AS A RESULT OF YOUR ATTEMPTS TO BE MORE RESPECTFUL TO HER OR HIM?

2. WHAT CHANGES DID YOU NOTE IN YOUR CHILD'S ATTITUDE TOWARD YOU?

3. CAN YOU THINK OF YET ANOTHER WAY THAT YOU COULD ENHANCE RESPECT? IF SO, WHAT?

ACTION PAGE 8

Think back once again to your own childhood, and recall a time when an adult in your life expressed love to you. Maybe it was a parent; maybe a grandparent, or another relative, or a friend. Maybe the expression was verbal; maybe it was nonverbal.

1. DESCRIBE THE EXPERIENCE:

2. HOW DID YOU FEEL?

To help you remember your expressions of love to your child or children, fill in the following chart:

CHILD'S NAME	YOUR EXPRESSION	YOUR CHILD'S RESPONSE

8

Responsibility and Discipline

The mother who spoils her child fattens a serpent.

SPANISH PROVERB

There was a young man who was desperate to work. He had never had a job before, though he was twenty-seven years old, and his parents were still supporting him financially. But they had finally had enough of his dependency, as well as their own overprotection, and had given him three months to find a job. When he saw, after ten weeks, that they were serious about pushing him out of the nest, he began seriously pounding the pavement for work.

He failed. Since he had never been taught to do things for himself, he had not developed the skills needed to find a job. As usual, however, his father came to his rescue and called a friend in the construction business. His son ended up with a well-paying job driving a dump truck.

On the first day of his first job, the young man backed the dump truck over an embankment. When the foreman asked how he could have done such a reckless thing, the young man replied, "Well, nobody told me not to."

This chapter and the next will offer some tried-and-true ways of handling problems and misbehavior when they occur in the family. But this chapter is also about something much more basic to the development of your child's ability to thrive in a democratic society. It is about *responsibility*.

Some Basic Questions About Responsibility

To make sure you understand the basic concepts associated with responsibility, I'll begin by posing and answering some fundamental questions about it.

What is responsibility? Here is a definition of responsibility:

Responsibility is a process of making choices and then accepting the consequences of those choices.

As human beings, we cannot avoid making choices; choices of every conceivable variety are presented to us daily and hourly. It is our attitude toward the consequences of our own choices that determines whether we are responsible or not.

How much responsibility for the course of our own lives do we accept? If the answer is less than total responsibility, then we are cheating ourselves. The more responsible we become, the more effective and satisfied with our circumstances we also become.

Why do we avoid responsibility if this is so? Because we are afraid of being blamed or punished for making mistakes.

Who would blame or punish us? Sometimes it is the critical people with whom we live and work. But even their criticism would be harmless if not for the fact that we blame and punish ourselves the hardest.

Where did we learn this self-criticism? Most of us learned it a long time ago from our parents, many of whom believed in being autocratic or permissive and in the blame and criticism that go with these styles.

How do we avoid responsibility? We blame others for our mistakes and failures, or we blame circumstances, because it is too painful to accept responsibility ourselves and then suffer the self-criticism we insist on dishing out. We say, "You made me late," or "You made me angry." Or we justify our failings: "Being late isn't such a big deal"; "I have a bad temper"; "I'm a Leo"; "I'm an alcoholic"; "I'm just no good"; "Nobody told me not to."

What happens when we avoid responsibility? The problem with avoiding responsibility for our mistakes is that we fail to learn from our experiences. We then continue to make the same mistakes in similar situations, backing our dump truck over the embankment and hoping that someone else will take the responsibility for us.

What happens when we accept responsibility? The most effective and the most satisfied people have learned how to deal with choices and accept responsibility for whatever happens as a result. If the consequence is a good one, then they have a good model for making a similar choice in the future. If the consequence is bad, then they will know better next time. Either way, they learn and they grow. And this is how children learn and grow, too.

How can we prepare children for responsible adulthood? The first step is to resist the temptation to blame and punish children for their mistakes and misbehavior. These techniques actually influence children to avoid responsibility—to blame and justify. This chapter is about other methods of disciplining children, methods that teach responsibility while they handle problems. In this chapter, you will learn some effective methods to help your child grow in his or her ability to make responsible choices. But first, let's look at the circumstances under which choices are made.

Freedom and the Limits to Freedom

We can only make choices when we have the freedom to choose, because if we are *not* free to choose, then we have to assume that someone else has already made the choices for us. Freedom to choose is an essential condition for choice.

There is a famous story among educators about a little boy in kindergarten who had a wonderful imagination. When the teacher said it was time to paint, he imagined all the wild animals that he would draw—lions, tigers, elephants, professional wrestlers. But then the teacher said, "Today, we are going to draw flowers."

Undaunted, the little boy imagined all the gloriously colored flowers that he would draw—red ones and yellow ones, some with purple and blue. But then the teacher said, "We're going to draw them like this." And the teacher drew a single brown flower with a green stem.

The little boy complied and drew his flower as the teacher had instructed. So it went all year long. The teacher always told the class how and what to draw.

That summer, the little boy and his family moved to another city and to a new school. When the teacher there announced that it was time for art, the little boy just sat there. All the other boys and girls began drawing, but he just waited. Finally, the teacher came over to his desk and asked the little boy why he wasn't drawing. "What should I draw?" he asked.

"Anything that you want," replied the teacher.

The little boy waited a few moments and then began to draw—a brown flower with a green stem.

As this sad story demonstrates, children need freedom if they are going to learn to make choices. On the other hand, there is no such thing as unlimited freedom to make choices. Every choice is hedged with restrictions: we cannot choose to use resources that we do not have; we cannot choose to deal with imaginary circumstances. The limits to freedom of choice are severe in some cases and lax in others. In making any choice, it is important to know where the limits are.

There is another story about a little boy who was sitting on the beach. His mother asked him, "What are you doing?"

"Watching the waves roll in," said the little boy.

"What have you learned?" asked his mother.

"That I can't stop the waves from rolling in," he said.

"And how does that make you feel?" asked his mother.

"Relieved," replied the little boy.

Just as children need and want freedom, they also find relief in knowing that there are limits to their freedom and power.

Autocratic parents give their children almost no freedom to make choices. They believe that since their children are inexperienced at knowing where the limits are, they must make the choices for them, thus saving their children the pain of poor choices. This method has severe disadvantages, not the least of which is that it stifles a child's ability to handle responsibility. These children eventually rebel against harsh and restrictive suppression of their growth, but are still inexperienced at making choices on their own.

Permissive parents, perhaps in reaction to their own autocratic upbringing, follow a model that resembles anarchy, allowing their children unlimited freedom, unlimited permission to do whatever they want. Yet, because they are never held responsible for the results of

GIVE CHILDREN CHOICES (Freedom Within Expanding Limits)

AGE 1–5	AGE 6–12	AGE 13–17
"Would you like orange juice or grapefruit juice this morning?"	"Would you like to help me do the grocery shopping?"	"Would you be willing to help out by planning and cooking dinner one night each week?"
"Can you put this away yourself or would you like some help?"	"Do you prefer to set 'homework time' for before dinner or afterward?"	"Now that you're getting up yourself in the morning, we think that you can also handle setting your own bedtime."

their choices, children do not learn responsibility any better in these circumstances than they do in an autocratic home.

Fortunately, as we have already seen, the democratic method is a middle ground between the permissiveness of anarchy and the oppressiveness of autocracy. Democratic parents are acutely conscious of their children's need for freedom, but freedom within well-defined limits. They allow children freedom of movement and freedom of choice within the limits that are appropriate for their age and abilities. One-year-old children might be allowed to make only one choice out of a multitude of choices made for them each day. Children of nine may be able and permitted to make more than half of their own choices, and adults of eighteen may make all of their own choices responsibly. This is freedom within expanding limits, and it is an essential concept in being an active parent. Through it, children gradually learn to set their own limits in accordance with the nature of the society in which they live. Children learn responsibility.

How do parents teach their children so valuable a skill as this? They teach it day by day, by giving choices and by dealing creatively with family conflicts and problems, using some of the simple but powerful tools this chapter will teach you.

A word of caution: Don't get carried away and make everything a choice. Sometimes children want and need a firm but friendly decision from a parent. This is particularly true in matters of health and safety. Later, in the section on "I" messages, you will learn some effective methods of providing limits *without* choices.

A Model for Handling Problems

How you handle the inevitable conflicts and problems of family life determines whether they are solved or get worse. The skills that you use also determine much of your family's satisfaction and what your child learns about responsibility and cooperation from the experience.

The chart below depicts a successful method of dealing with family problems. We will discuss "I" messages and logical and natural consequences in this chapter. Active communication (Chapter 9) and the family council meeting (Chapter 10) will be covered later.

If there is a problem, first determine WHO OWNS IT.	
IF THE PARENT OWNS IT:	**IF THE CHILD OWNS IT:**
1. First try sending the child an "I" MESSAGE.	**1.** Sometimes do nothing and allow the NATURAL CONSEQUENCES to occur.
2. If the problem continues, then set up LOGICAL CONSEQUENCES.	**2.** Let the child handle it, but offer support through ACTIVE COMMUNICATION.
3. As a last resort, deal with the problem in a FAMILY COUNCIL.	**3.** As a last resort, deal with the problem in a FAMILY COUNCIL.

Determining Who Owns the Problem

Who owns the problem? may seem a strange question to ask. What does it mean to "own" a problem, anyway? Owning in this case means accepting responsibility for handling the problem. Some problems—usually a child's misbehavior—belong to you, as parent and leader, to handle. Other problems are your child's responsibility, and he or she should be shown respect by being allowed to handle them.

Autocratic parents act as if they own all the problems in the family and should make all the choices. But even democratic parents are tempted to take responsibility for problems that don't belong to them at all—problems that, in fact, belong to their children. Children grow in responsibility by taking charge of their own problems, so it is a good idea to determine, once a problem surfaces, just who owns it.

You can quickly determine who owns the problem by asking these kinds of questions:

- Who is this behavior (or situation) interfering with directly?

- Who is raising the issue or making the complaint?

- Whose purposes are being thwarted?

- Who has the negative feelings?

That person usually owns the problem. Here are some examples:

SITUATION	WHO OWNS PROBLEM?	WHY?
Children are giggling and noisy at dinner at a restaurant.	Parent	Parents are eating in a public place and the children's noise is disturbing other patrons and interfering with parents' enjoyment of their meal.
Your daughter drives the car into the garage too fast.	Parent	It is the parents' responsibility to train their children to use automobiles safely; this situation isn't safe.
Your daughter doesn't like her sister going into her room without her permission.	Child	Siblings are entitled to have a relationship with each other without parental intervention. They need to learn to work out together how they can best get along.
Your child complains that the teacher picks on him.	Child	Children have relationships with other adults. They need to learn how to relate with them on their own.
Your child has a temper tantrum in the supermarket.	Parent	The child's behavior is interfering with the parent's purpose—that is, shopping.
Your child doesn't complete a homework assignment.	Child	Schoolwork is the child's responsibility, not the parent's. The child has to deal with the teacher if his or her work isn't done.

If your child owns the problem, then you can let the child handle it, while providing the child all the support he or she needs. We will discuss some support techniques in the next chapter. On the other hand, if you own the problem, then you must handle it with your child, and in such a way that the child learns and grows in responsibility. In this case, I recommend two basic methods. One is a communication technique called sending "I" messages. The other is a discipline skill called setting up logical consequences. Both have been found to work much better than traditional punishment methods. Let's look at each.

Sending "I" Messages

The concept of "I" messages was developed by psychologist Thomas Gordon in his famous PET program. "I" messages are so called because their sender uses the pronoun "I" to take responsibility for his or her feelings. "I" messages are powerful tools to use in family interactions, because they do these things:

- They allow a parent to say how he or she feels about the child's behavior without blaming or labeling the child.

- They create a situation in which the child is inclined to hear what the parent is saying, because it is expressed in a nonthreatening way.

- They convey clearly to the child one consequence (the parents' feelings) of the child's behavior.

- They put the emphasis on the parent and his or her feelings, not on the child and the child's personality.

- When delivered clearly and firmly, "I" messages often influence the child to change his or her behavior.

"I" messages are effective only when the problem belongs to the parent (or to the person sending the message). An "I" message is a first-line attempt at dealing with a problem; if the problem remains after the "I" message, then the parent can move to setting up logical consequences.

Sending an "I" message has four steps:

1. Name the behavior or situation. This part of the message is a description of the issue at hand, and involves no judgments. It begins with "When you . . ."

2. Say specifically how you feel about the effect of the situation on you. This part beings with "I feel . . ."

3. State your reason. Say how the situation or behavior interferes with your wants or purposes. This part begins with "because . . ."

4. Say what you want done. This part begins with "I want . . ." or "I would like . . ."

    Here is an example of an "I" message:

When you don't finish the kitchen jobs you agreed to do,
I feel you're being unfair to me,
Because the kitchen I have to work in is messy and smelly.
I would like you to stick to your agreements and finish your job.

    As you probably recognize, by using an "I" message, you—the parent—accept responsibility for your own feelings. This makes the confrontation much easier for the child to hear than the usual "you" message that's built into a statement like this: "*You* make me so angry when you don't do your job."

Although each element of the "I" message is important, you don't have to use this exact form. Choose words that fit your own style. But be on guard—especially if you are a man—against leaving out the feeling part. If you are a woman, be on guard against leaving out the "I would like" part.

Another word of caution. Try to avoid using *angry* as your feeling word too often. Look for feelings that may lie beneath your anger—for example, *hurt* or *afraid*. This is especially true if you are already in a power struggle with your child. Your "anger" may be interpreted by your child as a victory for him or her, and your "I would like" statement may be taken as a challenge. But for the majority of situations, "I" messages work surprisingly well.

CASE 18

If you remember the problem Jason's mother had getting her son to come to the dinner table (Case 3), you can appreciate her frustration when Jason wolfed down his meal in five minutes and bolted from the table. She decided that since *she* was the person bothered by the situation, it must be her problem. Since she owned the problem, it was her responsibility to take some action in handling it. She decided to use an "I" message.

She carefully thought out what she would say. That night at dinner when Jason began his sprint from the table, she was ready.

"Jason," she said firmly, "when you leave the table before everyone is finished, I feel shortchanged because we miss your company. I want you to sit down until dinner is over."

When Mrs. Bradford told me about the incident, she was ecstatic. "His head spun around like it was on a string. It was like it was the first time that he had ever heard me. He sat down without a complaint and stayed the entire meal." To make matters even better, she had been sure to encourage Jason's cooperation by telling him after the meal how much she had enjoyed his company.

Comment: The structure of the "I" message helps parents be both firm and friendly at the same time. When parents are either wishy-washy or enraged they turn their children off, producing a medical disorder that we jokingly call "parent-deafness." Jason's mother's "I" message helped him overcome this age-old malady. He heard her clearly and recognized from her words and tone that she meant what she said.

Using Logical Consequences

When children do not respond to the needs of a situation or a family rule after a polite request or an "I" message, the parent, as leader in the family, must use discipline. I've already presented the case against using punishment as a discipline tool. Letting your child experience the logical consequences of his or her behavior is a much more effective means of discipline.

What is the value of consequences? Children learn responsibility when they are first allowed to choose how to behave. Once they have made a choice about how to behave, it is important for them to experience the consequences of that choice. When they experience the consequences of misbehavior, the lesson they learn is more powerful than any lecture or arbitrary punishment.

Logical consequences are results that you, as a parent, deliberately choose and establish to show your child what logically follows when he or she violates family values or social requirements. Here are some examples of logical consequences:

- When Danny comes home too late for supper, he must eat cold leftovers, alone, and he must clean up his own dishes.

- When Susan does not get up when her mother calls her in the morning, she must get dressed in the car while being driven to school.

Logical consequences are not the same thing as punishment, even though the child may experience both as unpleasant. Here are some differences between the two.

LOGICAL CONSEQUENCES . . .	PUNISHMENT . . .
. . . are demonstrations of what logically follows from misbehavior	. . . is an arbitrary retaliation for misbehavior.
. . . are intended to show children how to behave responsibly.	. . . is intended to impose parents' will on children.
. . . are administered in a firm and friendly manner, without anger or hostility.	. . . is too often delivered in an atmosphere of anger and resentment.

Practice recognizing the difference between punishment and logical consequences with the following examples.

Write LC or P beside each of the following items to show whether you think they are examples of logical consequences or punishment.*

1. When Paul stays out later than the agreed-upon curfew, he must do twenty-five pushups.

2. When Tommy paints dirty words on the sidewalk, he must clean all the paint away with turpentine and a scrub brush.

3. When Mollie refuses to eat her supper, she is made to stand in the corner for thirty minutes.

4. When Art breaks his mother's hand mirror, he must pay for it out of his allowance.

It's important to give children choices regarding the consequence. As we have emphasized, learning how to handle responsibility is learning how to make choices. Children always choose, given the opportunity, and the consequences of those choices teach them how to make similar choices in the future. You can help your child make choices by showing her or him that misbehavior is one of the choices, but it brings with it logical consequences. You should outline and emphasize the other choices for your child.

Keep in mind that often children misbehave because they just do not know better. "I" messages are an excellent way to provide them with an explanation about *why* something they are doing needs to be changed, so you should use "I" messages before setting up logical consequences. Once your child knows better, you need not give extra explanations before giving choices. I will now describe in detail how to use logical consequences with your child.

Outline the choices. You can give your child two types of choices:

- *Either-or choices:* Phrase these choices like this: "Either you may _____, or you may _____. You decide."

- *When-then choices:* Phrase these choices like this: "When you have _____, then you may _____."

Here are some examples of either-or choices:

- *Katherine sings and babbles loudly while her parents try to talk.* "Katherine, either you may play quietly here, or you may go to your room.

*Answers: **1.** P **2.** LC **3.** P **4.** LC

You decide, dear." (Notice that the logical consequence of continuing to distract the parents is to give up the pleasure of their company.)

■ *Donny is teasing the puppy.* "Donny, you may either pet the puppy gently like this [demonstrating] or you may take him back to his box. You decide." (Notice that the logical consequence of continuing to tease the puppy is to lose the privilege of playing with him.)

Here are some examples of when-then choices:

■ *Maria is watching TV when she has been asked to make up her bed.* "Maria, when you have made up your bed, then you may watch TV." (Notice that the logical consequence of Maria's not making up her bed is losing the privilege of watching TV.)

■ *Tom is about to leave for the swimming pool, ignoring his regular Saturday task of mowing the lawn.* "Tom, when you have mowed the lawn, then you may go swimming."

NOTE: When offering a when-then choice, sequence the choices so that the less desirable activity is mentioned *before* the more desirable one. This "work-before-play" sequence has worked so well for so long that psychologists often refer to it as "Grandma's rule."

It is better not to couch choices in negative terms: "Don't do that, or else . . ." When children hear such a choice, they often take it as a challenge. Such a negative choice sounds very much like a threat of punishment, and it often promotes a power struggle. Providing the choice in positive terms as often as possible is much less confrontational. Here are some examples of how *not* to express a choice:

■ "Donny, stop teasing the puppy, or I'll make you take him back to his box."

■ "Katherine, stop that racket or else go to your room."

■ "Tom, you may not go swimming until you have mowed the grass."

Give the choice only one time; then act. If you child continues to misbehave after you have given the choices, then you should interpret the continued misbehavior as the choice. That choice carries with it some consequences, and you, the parent, must act to put the consequences into effect. Don't give the choices a second time without first putting the consequences into effect. The child must see that the choice results in the consequence, and the lesson must be clear, or its value is diminished. Here are some examples:

- Katherine has been offered the choice of playing quietly in the living room while her parents talk, or going to her room to play alone if she continues to sing and babble loudly. If Katherine chooses to continue to misbehave, the parent can say, "I see you've decided to play in your room for now. 'Bye. See you later."

  If Katherine doesn't leave, the parent can firmly but kindly take her hand and escort her to her room to play. Crying or protesting on Katherine's part should not change the parent's behavior. Katherine chose to continue loud babbling and singing, and she now understands the consequences of her choice. She will get the chance to choose again later.

- Tom has been told he may go swimming only after he has finished his regular Saturday chore of mowing the grass. He protests and tries to get the parent to relent, or at least to postpone the yard work until later. The parent can say, "I'm sorry, Tom, but since you have chosen not to mow the grass, that means you have decided not to go swimming."

Allow your child to try again later. Since you want your child to learn from the consequences of his or her choices, you must provide an opportunity to try again, but only after the child has experienced the consequences of the first choice. Here are some examples:

- Katherine has been taken to her room to play, since she chose to be disruptive in the living room. After she plays in her room for awhile, she may return. If she does so, the parent can say something encouraging like this: "Good to have you back. We're glad you decided to play quietly."

- Tom stops his protest and mows the lawn. The parent can say (with a friendly smile), "I see you have decided to go swimming after all."

If your child repeats the misbehavior after experiencing the consequences, then he or she is testing you to see whether you mean what you say. You can meet this challenge by letting the consequences operate a little longer after the second try, and still longer after the third try, and so on. Here are some examples:

- If Katherine has come back to the living room to try again, yet chooses once more to misbehave, the parent can require her to stay in her room for a longer period (perhaps twenty minutes, this time). If a third time becomes necessary, Katherine can be required to stay in her room still longer.

- If Tom starts for the swimming pool again next week without mowing the lawn, the parent can say, "It seems to me that you've decided not to swim today. We can try again tomorrow."

Avoid turning logical consequences into punishment. Using logical consequences to threaten children or to impose your demands on them is a mistake. This is really the same thing as punishment, and children respond as though they were being punished. It is important for your attitude to be friendly and supportive when you apply consequences. Here are some final tips:

- Don't set up choices or apply logical consequences in an angry manner. Your anger, in itself, can be punishing to the child.

- Whenever possible, discuss the problem with the child, and ask what he or she thinks the logical consequences might be. Sometimes the problem can be solved just by this kind of discussion; children often have much to offer. In addition, when children help set the consequence beforehand, parents usually have less trouble enforcing it later.

- Make sure the consequences you decide upon are really logical. Children see the justice of logical consequences, and they usually accept them without resentment. But if a consequence you decide upon is not related to your child's misbehavior, it will seem arbitrary and punishing.

- Offer choices that are acceptable to you, the parent. Do not set up your child by first giving a choice and then getting angry at your child for choosing it. For example, Danny's mother says, "Danny, either eat your peas or leave the table." As Danny begins to leave his seat, his mother slaps the table and says angrily, "You sit down this minute, young man, and finish those peas!"

- Expect your child to *test*. This means that most children continue to misbehave for a while even after the logical consequences are in place. They are testing to see if we are really going to do what we say that we are going to do. Will we *act* or just talk? It is the *active* parent who teaches. The more inconsistent you have been in the past, the more your child will test.

CASE 19

Susan Bradford, Lisa's and Jason's younger sister, has a tendency to lose things. When it became apparent that Susan had lost her only winter coat last December, her mother and father were faced with a dilemma. Should they let Susan go without a coat—and perhaps get sick—or should they do what they usually did, and buy her a new coat. Fortunately, they realized that they had a third choice. They could use a logical consequence to help teach Susan responsibility for her belongings.

The Bradfords first discussed this between themselves, then approached Susan. "Honey," her father began, "what are we going to do about that missing coat?"

"I don't know," said Susan.

"Well," said her mom, "it's too cold to go without one, unless you can grow some fur."

Everyone laughed, and her mom continued. "Seriously, we need to buy a new one, and your dad and I feel that you can help pay for it."

"Get serious, Mom!" Susan exclaimed. "I can't afford a coat!"

"We'd like you to help," added her dad. "It would show us that you can handle some responsibility for your mistakes."

"Right," added her mother. "We could pay for it, and you could pitch in and repay us two dollars a week from your allowance until spring. Or would you rather us give you a new coat as your Christmas present?"

Susan's eyes rolled up to the ceiling as if she were suddenly nauseated. "Okay. I'll pay two dollars per week."

"Great!" said her dad. "We can go shopping after dinner for a new coat."

Comment: Susan's mom and dad were firm and friendly as they developed an either-or choice for her: *either* pitch in *or* take the coat as your Christmas present. Inviting Susan to help find alternatives showed their respect for her as a thinking person, as did their refusal to bail her out. Their active use of logical consequences will help Susan remember her belongings, as long as they follow through with the consequence, and do not raise her allowance or otherwise let her squirm out of it.

NOTE: This story also demonstrates the value of giving your children an allowance as soon as they can count. When children are young, a small allowance with limited responsibilities (for example, a couple of dollars for snacks at a movie) is a good idea. As they get older, a larger allowance with more responsibilities is in order. Teenagers on a larger allowance might be handling their own recreation, lunches, and even clothing. Discussion between you and your child is the best way to determine the specifics.

EIGHT DO'S OF LOGICAL CONSEQUENCES

---

1. Give the child a choice:
   - either/or
   - when/then
2. Make sure the consequence is logical.
3. Ask the child to help.
4. Give choices that you can live with.
5. Keep your tone firm and friendly.
6. Give the choice only once, then act.
7. Expect testing.
8. Allow the child to try again later.

When Misbehavior Pays Off

We have talked about a specific type of consequence you can use very deliberately to guide your child. But in fact, if you think back to the parent-child behavior cycle described in Chapter 4, you'll realize that every time you respond to your child, your behavior is a consequence. How children generally choose to be influenced by parental behavior is called the balance of consequences:

- If children derive benefits from the consequences of misbehavior, they will continue that misbehavior.

- If children derive no benefits from the consequences of misbehavior, they will change the misbehavior.

In other words—kids only do what works.

In Chapter 4, I also presented the four goals of behavior and the four mistaken approaches that children sometimes use. Why do children often continue their mistaken approaches (that is, misbehavior) even when parents remind, nag, or punish? The answer is simple: they get some benefit from these consequences. Since this benefit or payoff balances the negative aspect of the parents' behavior, the misbehavior continues to be worthwhile. The chart on page 115 gives some examples.

When you are trying to change your child's mistaken approach or misbehavior, it is important to ask, "How can I avoid making this misbehavior pay off?" Often this means doing the unexpected—sending

GOAL	MISTAKEN APPROACH	PARENT'S BEHAVIOR (the negative consequence)	CHILD'S PAYOFF	CHILD'S UNDERLYING BELIEF
Belonging	Seeking undue attention	Reminding, nagging, scolding.	Undue attention	"I got what I wanted—to keep them busy with me."
Power	Rebellion	Gets angry and gives in.	Power	"See how powerful I am; I got my way!"
Power	Rebellion	Gets angry and fights.	Power	"See how powerful I am; I made them mad!"
Protection	Seeking revenge	Punishes/hurts back.	Justifies child's behavior	"I have a right to hurt them; they hurt me!"
Withdrawal	Avoidance	Gives up.	Avoidance	"Now I won't have to try, and risk disappointing them even more."

an "I" message instead of nagging; removing yourself from the situation before you get too angry; setting up a logical consequence instead of issuing a threat, just to name a few.

Encouragement and Consequences: A Powerful Combination

It has probably become evident to you that I do not view discipline as a dirty word. In fact, democracy, as well as the democratic parent, would be ineffective without it. Employing logical consequences is both a more effective and a more respectful form of discipline than punishment. But it does take practice to become skilled. After all, an autocratic parent can have one punishment that fits any misbehavior. Using logical consequences requires you to think logically in each situation and find a consequence that is logically related to the misbehavior. As you gain experience with this technique, you will find it easier to come up with such consequences.

As effective as this method can be as a discipline tool, it works much, much better when it is complemented with systematic encouragement. For example, in Case 19, the goal of Susan's parents is to teach their daughter to remember her belongings (a step toward the long-term goal of responsibility). They have set up a logical consequence (Susan helps pay for lost items) to help achieve this goal. But how much more powerful the lesson will be if they also find ways to encourage Susan when she *does* remember her belongings! This double approach is what we might call a democratic version of the old "carrot and stick." And without the pitfalls of reward and punishment, it is a very powerful combination indeed.

Letting Natural Consequences Follow

We have discussed two methods of teaching your child responsibility when *you* own the problem. Let's now see one way for you to help promote responsibility when *your child* owns the problem. Natural consequences are the experiences that follow naturally (that is, without parents' intervention) from what children choose to do or not to do. Some examples:

- The natural consequence of touching a hot object is a painful burn.
- The natural consequence of going outside on a cold day without mittens is cold hands.
- The natural consequence of leaving a bicycle out in the rain is a rusty chain.

While they are useful tools, natural consequences cannot *always* be used as teachers. In situations like the following, parents cannot rely on natural consequences to teach their children responsibility:

- When the natural consequence may be catastrophic: the natural consequence of playing near the swimming pool may be to fall in and drown.
- When the consequence is so far in the future that the child cannot make the connection: the natural consequence of not brushing teeth may be tooth decay, but not today, or tomorrow, or next week.
- When there simply are no natural consequences to an act: there is no natural consequence to reading a book at the dinner table, but most parents discourage their children from going so.

Some situations call for you to take direct action, usually through an "I" message or a logical consequence. But many of life's lessons can be taught more effectively if you let your child experience the natural consequences of his or her choice without interference.

There is a story about a master who sent his teenage student into the woods to observe a cocoon. The young man watched as the butterfly's wings began to break through their silken fibers. He watched and waited and watched and grew impatient. Unable to simply observe any longer, he reached in and helped the butterfly out of the cocoon.

The tender butterfly flew a few feet and then spiraled to the earth and died. The student, his eyes wet with tears, hurried back to the master and asked what had happened. The master explained, "When you reached in and opened the cocoon, you deprived the butterfly of the chance to strengthen its wings in the struggle."

Many parents find it difficult to allow their children to experience the bumps and bruises of childhood. Like the teenage student, they want to reach in and rescue. But sometimes, doing nothing is the best thing to do. Children learn best from direct experience, and mild mishaps during childhood are a small price to pay for an education in responsibility that can prevent major tragedies in adulthood.

CASE 20

When Susan Bradford lost things, her mother's tendency used to be to constantly remind Susan *not* to forget things, to scold her when she did forget, and then to replace the lost object. But when Mrs. Bradford stepped back and analyzed the situation a little more objectively, she realized that Susan was getting a lot of undue attention for her forgetfulness. In addition, her behavior was discouraging, and Susan was not experiencing the consequences of her own actions. This all added up to Susan's lack of responsibility.

Mrs. Bradford decided to begin by encouraging Susan. She showed confidence in Susan's ability by telling her, "I've decided that all my nagging is really disrespectful. You've got good sense, and I'm sure that if I let you handle it yourself, you'll do fine."

A few days later, Susan asked her mom if she had seen her softball glove. Her mother said no, and resisted the temptation to lecture. Instead, she said encouragingly, "I hope you find it, dear."

Two days laters Susan found it in the back yard where she had left it. Unfortunately, it had rained, and to make matters worse, a dog had chewed it like a bone. Although it was still usable, Susan thought it was "gross" and asked her mom to get a new one.

Mrs. Bradford again refrained from lecturing or stabbing Susan with an "I-told-you-so." Instead, she said, "Gee, honey, I'm sorry your glove is such a mess. But I've decided to let you handle your property, and I wouldn't be doing that if I ran out and bought you another glove."

Comment: Susan's mother uses excellent judgment in letting her daughter learn from the natural consequences of her actions. Such experiences will help Susan learn to take better care of her belongings. Her mother's encouraging attitude makes it difficult for Susan to sidestep her own responsibility by blaming her mother or engaging in a fight.

ACTION PAGE 9

Think of recent problem that *you* own with one of your children—that is, a misbehavior that you want to change.

---

1. HOW DID YOU FEEL THE LAST TIME THE PROBLEM OCCURRED?

Annoyed   Angry   Hurt   Helpless

---

2. WHAT WAS YOUR CHILD'S RESPONSE TO YOUR METHOD OF HANDLING THE PROBLEM?

---

3. WHAT WAS YOUR CHILD'S MISTAKEN APPROACH?

Using your answers from 1 and 2, what was your child's mistaken approach (seeking undue attention, rebellion, seeking revenge, or avoidance)? (Refer to the chart on page 54 if you need help deciding.)

---

4. HOW DOES YOUR OWN BEHAVIOR PAY OFF YOUR CHILD'S MISTAKEN APPROACH?

ACTION PAGE 9 (continued)

5. SUGGEST ONE LOGICAL CONSEQUENCE THAT YOU CAN USE.

a. Either _____, or _____.

b. When you have _____, then you may _____.

6. WHAT SIGNS OF IMPROVEMENT WILL YOU ENCOURAGE

Remember, any progress should be encouraged.

7. WHEN WILL YOU PUT YOUR PLAN INTO ACTION?

8. EVALUATE HOW IT'S GOING.

Encourage yourself. If it isn't going well, check the "Eight Do's of Logical Consequences" to find where you may be off. Try again—you didn't ride a bike so well your first time, either!

9

Winning
Cooperation

*The reason why we have two ears and
only one mouth is that we may listen
the more and talk the less.*

ZENO OF CITIUM

Active Parenting stresses three qualities—courage, responsibility, and cooperativeness—that summarize the aims of parenthood. Any parent can feel optimistic if his or her child is developing these three qualities. Once again, they are courage, responsibility, and cooperativeness.

Courage, as we discussed in Chapter 5, is the willingness to take a known risk for a known purpose. Parents can help their children learn courage by giving them large and steady doses of encouragement.

Responsibility, as we learned in Chapter 8, is the willingness to make choices and to accept the consequences of those choices. Parents can help their children learn responsibility by giving them choices to make and then letting them learn through the natural and logical consequences of those choices.

Cooperation is the major subject of this chapter and the next one, and what better time to teach cooperation than when your child has a problem. If you look back at the problem-handling chart on page 104 you'll notice that the first choice you have when your child owns a problem is to do nothing, allowing the natural consequences to teach responsibility. But you will want to support your child in handling problems more effectively sometimes. To do this requires good communication skills, which we will deal with in this chapter. Then, in Chapter 10, we will look at the basis of family cooperation, the family council meeting.

Communication: The Road to Cooperation

There was once a Roman galley on which all of the slaves were chained to their seats. One of the slaves, rowing to the beat of the drum, looked over at the slave next to him. He was horrified at what he saw. The other slave was drilling a hole in the bottom of the boat—under his seat.

"What in Jupiter's name are you doing?!" exclaimed the first slave.

"What's it to you?" replied the second. "I'm only drilling the hole under *my* seat."

The joke, of course, is that when you are riding in the same boat, it doesn't matter where the hole is; everyone is going to get wet. Nowhere is the same principle more evident than in a family. When one member in a family owns a problem, everyone in the family is going to feel the ripples.

When you are in it together, you have a real stake in each other's problems. There is also strength in numbers. By working together, two or more people can accomplish much more than each one could individually. When people cooperate, problems are usually resolved. Cooperation is a very powerful force, indeed.

Let's try a definition of cooperation:

Cooperation is two or more people working toward a common goal.

How powerful a force is cooperation? So powerful that it dwarfs its overemphasized cousin, competition, by comparison. In fact, competition is useful only in small doses. Too much of it, like yeast, ruins the whole thing. But cooperation, unleashed, builds democracies and creates civilizations.

When a problem belongs to the child, the parents have a unique opportunity to use good communication skills to help the child learn how to arrive at a solution. In so doing, they do not rob the child of the responsibility for handling his or her problem, nor of the courage necessary to do so. Through active communication between parent and child concerning a child's problem, the child learns that "two heads are better than one"—that when we solve problems cooperatively, better solutions happen. Problem solving as a team is an encouraging and validating experience, and it fosters a respect for cooperation.

Avoiding Communication Blocks

Just as the first step in learning to effectively encourage children is learning to avoid *dis*couraging them, the first step in effective communication is to learn to avoid blocking that communication. A communication block is any remark or attitude on the part of a listener that convinces the speaker that the listener isn't really listening. It obstructs the flow of the sharing that takes place in true communication. (Why should anyone continue sharing thoughts and feelings with someone who isn't really listening?) Here are some examples of ways that parents block communication:

- A child is sharing her outrage. Never mind whether the outrage is ugly or not; never mind whether the child is "right" or not. The parent can choose to listen to the content of the outrage and the feeling behind it, or decide to keep things under control by responding with "Don't talk back to me" or "Stop complaining." The parent has effectively blocked further communication.

- A child is sharing his fear about an upcoming test of his courage or ability. The parent can listen to the content of that fear and allow the child to express as much of it as possible, or try to talk the child out of his feelings by placating or distracting: "You usually come through okay." "It isn't really as bad as it seems." "Let's not worry about that; things will look brighter tomorrow." Why should a child continue sharing apprehensions with someone who says they are insignificant? The parent has blocked communication.

- A child is sharing her pain surrounding her difficulties with enemies or friends or teachers or other family members. The parent can listen to the content of that pain or moralize and play psychologist: "You're just jealous, that's all." "You should know better than to act that way." "You brought all this on yourself, you know."

Parents who construct these communication blocks usually do so with good intentions:

- Parents who *command* want to keep things under control.

- Parents who *give advice* want to influence the child with arguments or opinions.

- Parents who *placate* or *distract* with sweet words want to protect the child from the problem, and so try to get the child to think of something else.

- Parents who *play psychologist* want to analyze the child's behavior and explain the child's motives.

- Parents who *interrogate* want to get to the bottom of the story quickly, so that a solution can be found or responsibility placed.

- Parents who *moralize* want the child to deal with the problem in a way that they think is proper.

- Parents who *use sarcasm* feel that making the child feel silly or ridiculous will cause the child to see how wrong his or her attitudes and behavior are.

- Parents who *act like know-it-alls* believe their greater experience gives them the right and/or duty to give the child the correct answers.

None of these parents listens to the child. All of these parents block further communication by the things they say. The following case illustrates the discouraging effect that such communication blocks can have on children's ability to handle their problems.

CASE 21

Dr. Bradford was in the driveway tinkering with the engine of his car when he heard in the distance the voice of a boy crying. He looked up and turned as Jason rushed toward him, the level of his crying increasing into sobs. In his hands was a toy truck.

DR. BRADFORD: What's the matter, Jason?

JASON: Daddy, Jimmy hit me!

DR. BRADFORD: What in the world happened?

JASON: Jimmy pushed me down and I hurt my leg.

DR. BRADFORD: Jason, calm down, for heaven's sake. What did you do that made him hit you?

JASON: Nothing. I was just standing there and he pushed me!

DR. BRADFORD: Are you sure?

JASON: Yes, I promise! I didn't do anything to him.

DR. BRADFORD: Stop crying, Jason. Big boys don't cry. What are you going to do?

JASON: There's nothing I can do; he's bigger than me.

DR. BRADFORD: Stop crying, now. Act like a man. What you need to do is learn to stand up for yourself. Show him he can't push you around.

Jason looked scared and withdrew hesitantly from his father.

Comment: First of all, Dr. Bradford fails to recognize that this problem belongs to Jason. As he takes over, he blocks communication by interrogating ("What did you do that made him hit you?"); commanding ("Stop crying"); moralizing ("Big boys don't cry") and being a know-it-all ("What you need to do is . . ."). It's no wonder that Jason withdraws from his father in a hesitant, discouraged manner.

Not only does Jason's dad not help him solve his problem with Jimmy, he actually creates a second problem. Jason now has the additional problem of living with a father who thinks he is a wimp. Would you approach your dad with your next problem if you were Jason?

Practicing Active Communication

Active communication is a set of communication skills that parents can use to support children in handling their own problems. You can learn these five skills and steadily improve them with practice. They are (1) listening actively, (2) listening for feelings, (3) connecting feelings to content, (4) looking for alternatives/predicting consequences, and (5) following up.

Listening Actively

Most people hear, but how many really listen? When you listen fully, you are not just a passive receiver of information; you are an active participant in the communication process. You listen with your eyes as well as your ears, with your intuition as well as your thinking abilities. Your object in listening actively is to encourage your child to express what he or she thinks and feels. You can achieve this object by keeping your own talk to a minimum, giving your child your full attention, and acknowledging what you are hearing.

Keep your own talk to a minimum. Have you ever had the annoying experience of telling someone something important to you, only to have that person aggressively change the direction of the conversation, using your comments as a springboard for recounting a similar experience, thought, problem, circumstance? You may try to steer the conversation back your way, or you may give up. In any case, the interchange has become a competition, not a conversation, and when both people are talking, no one is listening. When you listen actively to your child, decide that you will keep your mouth closed, except to make occasional comments that keep the conversational ball rolling—your child's way.

Give your full attention. Have you ever been at a large gathering, telling something important to someone, only to find that your listener is not really listening to you? He or she may look at you, smile at appropriate times, and make brief comments here and there, but you can see the person's eyes wander away from you, occasionally lighting up when a familiar person passes by. It's disrespectful to listen that way to anyone, especially to your child. When you are listening actively to your child, you give him or her your full attention. If you cannot turn off the TV set, stop cooking, or drop the newspaper, then you can ask your child to wait until you have the time to listen. When you listen, the full focus of your attention should be on what your child is saying. A child who gets his or her parent's full attention usually feels encouraged by the attention alone, which says, "I care about you; you matter; I'm here to help."

Acknowledge what you are hearing. Active listening does not require absolute silence. When you are listening to your child, it helps to show that you are understanding, that you are taking it in. You can say something as simple as "I see" now and then, or even "Umm-hmm." You can ask questions that clarify what the child is saying, or you can summarize lengthy or complicated circumstances with something like, "Now let me see if I've understood this right. You and Billy were at the pond, and . . ." If you have misunderstood, your child has an opportunity to correct you with no harm done to the process. When you are hearing accurately, the stage is set for the next step.

Listening for Feelings

There are no *wrong* feelings, for either you or your children. There are certainly unpleasant feelings, which often suggest mistaken attitudes or perceptions, but feelings in themselves are neither wrong nor right. They simply *are,* and whether we like it or not, they influence us, and they act with a stronger force if we don't acknowledge and accept them. Acknowledging and accepting our feelings doesn't necessarily mean acting on them, only looking at them for information about our own response to a given situation, problem, or circumstance.

So acknowledging our feelings about a problem is often a first step in dealing with that problem. You can help your child learn to acknowledge his or her own feelings by listening for the feelings implied in what your child says. Sometimes children are unaware of their feelings, but may see the truth when their parents help them give those feelings a name.

Connecting Feelings to Content

Once you have actively listened to the content of what your child has to say, and once you have an idea of what the child is feeling, the next step is to reflect those feelings back to the child. You want to become what psychologist Chaim Ginot called an emotional mirror, so that your child can connect his or her feelings with the content of the problem. This reflection takes the form of a tentative statement like this:

■ "It sounds as though you might be resentful that Lonnie's score was better than yours."

The following chart shows how you can combine a feeling word with the content of what your child says to create a reflection—an active response that helps your child understand what he or she is feeling.

WHAT THE CHILD SAYS	FEELING WORD	WHAT THE PARENT SAYS
Mom, I'm *not* going to clean my dumb room!	Angry	You're angry that I want you to clean up your room.
I didn't catch the ball and and we lost the game.	Disappointed	Sounds like you're disappointed for missing the catch.
I don't like to smile. I hate these braces.	Embarrassed	You're embarrassed to smile with braces on your teeth.
Look at my fingerpainting	Pleased	You're really pleased with your painting.

Although the English language has hundreds of words that describe specific feelings, most people do not have very many on the tip of their tongue. As you practice looking for the right feeling word to reflect back to your child, you will find that your vocabulary increases and the job gets easier. To help with the process, I have compiled a list of 100 common feeling words for you to keep in mind.

100 Common Feeling Words			
WORDS THAT DESCRIBE PLEASANT FEELINGS		**WORDS THAT DESCRIBE UNPLEASANT FEELINGS**	
accepted	hopeful	afraid	jealous
adventurous	humble	angry	let-down
adequate	important	anxious	lonely
bold	joyful	ashamed	miserable
brilliant	loving	bashful	nervous
calm	lovely	bored	overwhelmed
caring	overjoyed	cautious	pained
cheered	peaceful	cheated	possessive
comfortable	peppy	concerned	provoked
confident	playful	defeated	pushed
content	pleased	defiant	rejected
daring	proud	disappointed	remorseful
eager	refreshed	discouraged	resentful
elated	relieved	down	shy
encouraged	satisfied	embarrassed	stupid
energetic	secure	envious	suspicious
excited	snappy	foolish	tired
fascinated	successful	frustrated	trapped
free	surprised	guilty	uncomfortable
full	sympathetic	hateful	uneasy
glad	tranquil	hesitant	unhappy
great	understood	hopeless	unloved
gutsy	warm	hurt	unsure
happy	wonderful	impatient	weary
high	zany	irritated	worried

Do not be concerned if you feel a little awkward at first. Most people do. The trick is to *reflect* the child's feeling without becoming a *parrot*. This takes practice (so you may as well put any perfectionism that you have away for a while). Avoid repeating your child's words verbatim. Use your own words and style, and above all, avoid those awful "You feel _____ because _____" sentence maps, or your child may have you arrested for impersonating a first-year counseling student.

Keep practicing. It is worth the effort. Children express feelings in one form or another. If you help them learn to express such unpleasant feelings as anger and hate with words, they will be less likely to express them through behavior—or misbehavior.

Looking for Alternatives/Predicting Consequences

Helping your child become an effective problem solver means helping her or him learn to look at alternative solutions and weigh the potential consequences. Many times, merely helping the child to connect feeling and content is enough to suggest a solution. But some problems are more difficult to deal with than others, and they require some action to remedy the situation. In many cases, you can begin by encouraging your child to look at the possible alternatives:

- "What can you do about that?"

- "What else can you try?"

After each alternative, you can help your child predict the consequences of that alternative:

- "What do you think would happen if you did that?"

It is better for the child to think of alternatives on his or her own, with your prompting. If your child cannot think of any, you can tentatively suggest some. Also, sharing your own experiences in similar situations can be helpful, as long as you don't use your testimonial as a goad, urging a specific course of action on your child. You can say something like:

- "I don't know what you will decide to do, but I remember a time when a friend of mine named Anita moved away without even saying goodbye. I felt hurt, then angry, then sad."

It is important to let your child have the final responsibility for deciding which alternative to choose, so refrain from telling him or her what to do. Children who figure out what to do feel a surge of self-esteem and learn to accept responsibility for their choices.

Following Up

Before you let go of your child's problem, you have one final step: to seek some kind of commitment from your child to a course of action. In other words, ask the child *what* he or she intends to do, and *when*. You can do this gently, knowing that even Einstein often needed to let new information incubate before his course of action became clear.

After your child has had an opportunity to handle the problem, you can follow up by beginning the active communication process over again:

- "How did it go with . . . ?"

In doing this, you not only help your child make sense of the total experience, but you also confirm that your interest was genuine.

Let's see how the active communication process works when all five steps are put together. In Case 21 we saw how Dr. Bradford let communication blocks interfere with his ability to help Jason handle a problem with Jimmy. An alternative to this approach, using active communication skills, might go as follows.

CASE 21 (ALTERNATIVE)

Dr. Bradford was in the driveway working on his car when he heard Jason's voice in the distance crying. He looked up and turned as Jason rushed toward him, the level of his crying increasing into sobs. In his hands was his toy truck.

DR. BRADFORD: What's the matter, Jason?

JASON: Daddy, Jimmy hit me!

DR. BRADFORD: What in the world happened?

JASON: Jimmy pushed me down and I hurt my leg.

DR. BRADFORD: Boy, I'll bet it hurts.

JASON: It does, it does.

DR. BRADFORD: Tell me again what happened.

JASON: I was just standing there holding my new truck, and he suddenly pushed me down. That dumb Jimmy, I hate him.

DR. BRADFORD: You sound very angry with him.

JASON: I am. He really hurt my leg.

DR. BRADFORD: Does it still hurt a lot?

JASON: Well, not so much now, but it sure did then!

DR. BRADFORD: I can imagine!

JASON: I didn't expect that at all.

DR. BRADFORD: You were surprised and scared when he pushed you.

JASON: Yeeeessss! I hate Jimmy. He's a rat.

DR. BRADFORD: I guess he hurt your feelings a great deal.

JASON: That damn Jimmy, I'm going to knock *him* down, and I hope he gets hurt!

DR. BRADFORD: That's one thing you could do. What do you think will happen if you do?

JASON: Well, he is bigger than me. He'd probably beat me up!

DR. BRADFORD: Can you think of anything else you might do?

JASON: I just won't play with him *ever again!*

DR. BRADFORD: Hmmm. Jimmy must have been pretty angry to have behaved like that.

JASON: I don't know. I was just standing there playing with my new truck. He said he wanted to see it. I told him that because it was brand new and expensive only I was allowed to play with it.

DR. BRADFORD: Oh, I see! Is that right?

JASON: Well, it is brand new.

DR. BRADFORD: I'm sure it is. You feel like he shouldn't play with it?

JASON: He might break it.

DR. BRADFORD: Is there any way you might feel comfortable with him playing with it?

JASON: Well, I suppose I could show him how and we could play together.

DR. BRADFORD: That sounds like a good idea to me.

JASON: Why should I, anyway?

DR. BRADFORD: There's no reason why you have to, but I imagine Jimmy would like to try it.

JASON: Well, maybe I'll ask him and maybe I won't.

DR. BRADFORD: Uh-huh. It's really your choice. I wonder what you'll decide.

JASON: I don't know.

DR. BRADFORD: Well, when you do decide, let me know. I'm anxious to hear how it works out.

The next day:

DR. BRADFORD: Jason, remember that talk we had yesterday about Jimmy?

JASON: Yeah.

DR. BRADFORD: I'm interested in what you finally decided to do.

JASON: Oh, I decided it was okay for him to play with my things if he's careful.

DR. BRADFORD: Great—I'm glad you worked it out.

ACTION PAGE 10

A. Practice recognizing the elements of active communication by reviewing Case 21 (Alternative) and writing examples of the five steps in the spaces below.

1. EXAMPLES OF HOW JASON'S DAD *LISTENED ACTIVELY:*

2. *FEELING* WORDS THAT HE USED:

3. HOW DID HE *CONNECT FEELINGS TO CONTENT?*

4. EXAMPLE OF *LOOKING FOR ALTERNATIVES* AND *PREDICTING CONSEQUENCES:*

5. HOW DID HE *FOLLOW UP?*

6. IF YOU WERE JASON, WOULD YOU SEEK OUT YOUR DAD IN THE FUTURE WITH A PROBLEM?

ACTION PAGE 10 (continued)

B. Now try the active communication process with your child, and analyze the effort.

---

1. WHAT WAS YOUR CHILD'S PROBLEM?

---

2. HOW DID YOU LISTEN ACTIVELY?

---

3. WHAT WERE SOME OF THE FEELING WORDS THAT YOU USED?

---

4. WHAT ALTERNATIVES AND CONSEQUENCES DID THE TWO OF YOU DISCOVER?

---

5. HOW DID THE PROCESS GO?

---

6. WHAT WERE THE WEAK POINTS? HOW WILL YOU IMPROVE NEXT ITEM?

---

7. HOW WILL YOU FOLLOW UP?

10

The Democratic Family in Action

Democracy is a very bad form of government, but all the others are so much worse.

ANONYMOUS

Contrary to the opening epigraph, I don't believe that democracy is really a bad form of government, just an imperfect one. It does have its problems, but with a cooperative and responsible effort on the part of its citizens (backed with a collective profile of courage), it can work splendidly. And it is up to each of us to make it work.

Because your purpose as an active parent is to instill in your children the qualities that will enable them to survive and thrive in a democracy, what better place to begin teaching democratic principles than in the family?! I have already discussed the importance of providing children with ways to influence their parents' decisions. This influence—this feeling on the part of children that their voices and their opinions make a difference—builds cooperation and responsibility and at the same time makes anger and rebellion less likely. In this chapter, we will look at a method of promoting cooperation by insuring that every family member's voice is heard. The method, the family council meeting, provides a forum in which all family members participate as equals and decisions are made by all members working together. The family council meeting also affords an excellent opportunity for parents and children to cooperatively find solutions to problems when the methods you learned in Chapters 8 and 9 have failed to change misbehavior.

Why Hold Regular Family Meetings?

I can think of six good reasons to hold family meetings on a regular basis. Maybe you can think of more.

1. *Cooperation.* Regular family meetings teach each person in the family that all of them are in the same boat and that the best way to decide how and where to steer is to share feelings and opinions until an agreement is reached.

2. *Responsibility.* Regular participation in family meetings teaches all family members that they must make the best choices they can make on behalf of the family, because they will all live with the consequences once the choices are made.

3. *Courage.* The family meeting is a laboratory for individual courage. Each family member learns how important it is to say what he or she really thinks and feels, even if it isn't shared by anybody else. The agenda also provides a specific opportunity for sharing encouragement.

4. *Love.* The family meeting helps love flow within the family circle, by letting family members share their feelings honestly with each other.

5. *Unity.* The family meeting is living proof that the family is a single body, tied together not only by kinship and daily association, but also by common purposes and a common way of dealing with problems and decisions.

6. *Education.* The family meeting teaches children a way of being in the world. Each family is a miniature society, and the social skills and attitudes that children develop within the family circle are the skills and attitudes that they will carry with them into their adult world. This is a place to teach democratic principles.

How to Get Started

As a parent, you will usually present the idea of having family meetings and get the meetings started. Here are some points to consider in setting up a family council meeting in your family.

Who should attend. Family meetings should include parents, children, and any others who live with the family, such as grandparents, uncles, or aunts. In other words, anyone who has a stake in decisions affecting the daily life of the family should be present at the family meetings. Some family members, however, may not be ready to discuss matters in a family meeting, or they may feel that a family council is not a good idea. Don't abandon the idea. Family meetings can still take place, if most family members agree to holding them. Those who do not attend the early meetings may decide to attend later, when they see the advantages and the results.

The single-parent household. Families affected by separation or divorce are still families and can hold family meetings even though one parent will not be participating. In those cases, it is important for the family to avoid discussing matters pertaining to the children's relationship with the absent parent. Those matters are owned by the children and the absent parent, and if there are problems, they should be handled by active communication, and away from the family meeting.

Time and place. Select a time and a place that is convenient and agreeable for everyone who will be attending. A good time for family meetings is Sunday afternoon, the beginning of the week. The family is more likely to be together at that time, and the past week can be reviewed, the forthcoming week anticipated. Meetings should be held in a place that is comfortable for all participants, preferably around a large table with room enough for everyone to pull up a chair.

The first meeting. The first family meeting should be a short one. It's an excellent idea to have only one item of business at this meeting: to plan an outing or a time for fun together right after the meeting. Later meetings can be longer, and follow a more extensive agenda.

Leadership roles. There are two leadership roles at family meetings. The chairperson keeps the discussion on track and sees to it that everybody's opinion is heard. The secretary takes notes during the meeting, writes up the minutes afterward, and then reads them at the next meeting. These two duties can be assumed by the parents at the first meeting. After that, the other family members should take turns, in an agreed-upon order, at being chairperson and secretary, so that no one person is in charge of things every time.

The Agenda for the Family Meeting

Here is an agenda for family meetings that works for many families. You can modify it to fit your circumstances.

1. *Compliments.* This is the time for family members to say thanks to each other for good deeds done or for help given during the past week, and to acknowledge strengths and encourage improvement.

2. *Minutes.* Last week's secretary reads the minutes of the last meeting.

3. *Old business.* Topics unfinished at the last meeting can be discussed further.

4. *Finances.* Many families have a special time for discussing financial matters. This is also a good time to pass out allowances.

5. *New business.* Discussion of new topics, complaints, or problems.

6. *Treat.* The meeting adjourns, but the family stays together for a game, an outing, or a dessert. This provides an opportunity to have fun together and to enjoy each other's company, and it gets the week off to a good start.

Most families find that the new business section of the family meeting works better if agenda items have been posted before the meeting. Tape a sheet of paper labeled "The Agenda" to the refrigerator or another convenient location. Write down any problems that a family member would like handled at the next family meeting.
For example:

The Agenda

1. Lisa comes into my room without knocking (Jason)

2. Raising allowances (Lisa)

3. Planning for the holidays (Mom)

Agenda items are handled in order at the next family meeting. Items not brought up before the meeting is over can be carried over to the next meeting. Many times an agenda item will have been handled by those involved before the meeting, so it can be dropped from the list.

One final benefit of having a written agenda is that it offers the parents an excellent way of staying out of children's fights. When a child tries to engage you in solving one of his or her problems, you can sympathetically suggest that it be put on the agenda for this week's meeting.

For example:

JASON: Mommy, Mommy! Lisa keeps coming into my room without knocking. Tell her to stop.

MRS. BRADFORD: Gee, honey, you sound pretty angry about that. Why don't you put it on the agenda for this week's family meeting?

Some Ground Rules for Meetings

Having ground rules for meetings helps keep them running smoothly. Make sure that everyone is aware of and has agreed to a set of rules like the following.

Each person has an equal voice. Although it is hard for parents to give up some of their authority, family meetings don't work very well unless each person has an equal voice in the decisions made. Each person, including small children, needs to feel that he or she will be heard and can make a difference in what the family decides to do. Children will not be enthusiastic about family meetings, nor will they derive much benefit from them, if the meetings are merely forums in which parents decide what everybody will do.

Everyone may share what he or she thinks about an issue. It is important that every person at the family meeting be encouraged to speak up and say whatever he or she thinks and feels about whatever question is on the table. In order to make decisions that are reasonable and fair to everyone, the family needs to hear what all the opinions and feelings are, even the negative ones. Parents should avoid expressing disapproval when their children share feelings or ideas that they disagree with or find unpleasant. If someone is too shy to speak up, he or she can be asked, gently, to offer an opinion.

Decisions are made by consensus. Consensus decision making means that when disagreement exists, the parties involved discuss the matter until all are agreed. It does *not* mean that a vote is taken and the majority rules. This would be impractical for two reasons. First, as I suggested earlier, any family with more children than parents would end up living at Disney World. Second, when a vote is taken, those in the minority sometimes feel resentful and may even sabotage the decision. It is much more effective to continue to work on a problem until a solution can be found that all can agree with. It may not be *anyone's* first choice, but if all can live with it, then progress is made. If an agreement cannot be reached in a family meeting, then one of two things happens: either the matter is tabled until the next meeting, or (if it urgently requires decision and action) the parents exercise their rights and make a decision.

All decisions hold until the next meeting. The decisions made at a family meeting should be carried out at least until the next meeting, when they can be discussed again. Complaints after the meeting about decisions made should always bring this rejoinder: "Bring it up again at the next family meeting."

Some decisions are reserved for parents. Holding meetings does not imply that the parents must always do whatever the children decide to do. Basic questions of health and welfare are parental responsibilities, and decisions regarding them are sometimes theirs alone to make. But discussion should always be allowed and encouraged. Sometimes a parent must tell the children of a decision already made. A parent who has been transferred by his or her company, for example, can't ask the children for approval. However, the children can be encouraged to share thoughts, concerns, and feelings about the move and to assist in the planning. Remember, democracy does not mean that you will get your way; it means that you will get your say.

Handling Problems in a Group

Recall from the chart on page 104 that as a last resort, family problems, regardless of who owns them, should be handled in the family council meeting. Take the following step-by-step approach to handling problems there.

1. *Define the problem.* The chairperson asks the person with the complaint or the issue to raise, to explain it, and then asks, "Is this still a problem?" If it is still a problem, then ask, "What happened?"

2. *Clarify the problem with active listening.* Family members ask clarifying questions and reflect back to the complainer what he or she is saying. At the end of this process, the chairperson gets agreement about the problem. For example, "So we all agree, don't we, that Susan borrowed Jason's tennis racquet without asking, and then it was stolen?" This is the time for family members to share thoughts and feelings about the problem.

3. *Generate possible solutions through brainstorming.* In brainstorming, family members think of all the possible solutions to a problem, no matter how silly or impractical the solutions may seem. This process is important because since one idea generates another, one person's silly idea may contain the germ of a practical solution. To keep the ideas flowing, no one is allowed at this point to criticize any of the ideas; they are simply tossed out into the group without evaluation. The secretary lists them on paper until no further ideas are forthcoming. Then each idea is discussed.

4. *Arrive at a decision through discussion.* Every person now has a chance to say what he or she thinks and feels about each possible solution. Ideas that are not acceptable to most are discarded, and discussion centers on one or two ideas that members consider feasible. Discussion continues until the group agrees on one solution.

5. *Put the decision into action.* The solution arrived at by brainstorming and discussion is put into effect.

How to Be an Effective Chairperson

Since you will be the chairperson for the first family meeting, you will set an example for the other family members to follow. When younger family members get their turn, share the following guidelines with them to help them in the role. Being chairperson means that you try to let everybody say what they want to say on each topic that the family talks about. You are like a referee, seeing that everybody gets his or her turn. Here's how you do it:

1. *Compliments.* Ask if anyone wants to express appreciation for the words or actions of someone during the past week. This is a good time for family members to thank each other for good deeds and encourage each other with compliments.

2. *Minutes.* Ask last week's secretary to read the minutes aloud. The minutes remind everyone of what happened at the last meeting.

3. *Old business.* Ask the family to talk about old business—any matter left unfinished at the last meeting. Let each person say what he or she wants to say, but remind people that they should not talk when someone else is talking. Use the techniques described on pages 138 and 139 to lead the group to a consensus.

4. *Finances.* Ask if anyone has any financial matters to bring up. After the family handles these matters, the parents should pass out allowances.

5. *New business.* Next, ask the family to talk about new matters on the agenda. Again, the problem-solving methods described on pages 138 and 139 will help you arrive at a consensus.

6. *Adjourn to a treat.* End the meeting by saying, "The meeting is adjourned." People get tired if meetings go on too long, so keep your meeting to the agreed time limit. Usually your family will have a game or a dessert after the meeting so that you can all have fun together.

How to Be an Effective Secretary

The secretary needs to do only three things at the family meeting:

1. Listen carefully to what is said.

2. Write down what is decided on each matter that is talked about.

3. Later (after the meeting) write a summary (called the minutes) of what is decided. Read the minutes aloud at the next meeting.

Here is what the minutes might look like:

Minutes of family meeting, June 22, 1987.

Chairperson was Susan. Secretary was Jason.

We decided that

1. We would go to Colorado this summer for vacation.

2. Susan would pay $3.00 out of her allowance for the lost rollerskating coupon.

3. We would wait until the next meeting to decide if we want to go on the next weekend hike in July with the Sierra Club.

CASE 22
(Transcript of the
Coleman family council
meeting)

Sunday evening, 7:00 P.M. Mrs. Coleman is at the dining room table.

MRS. COLEMAN: Okay, gang, 7:00. Time for family council.
(*Enter Mr. Coleman, Dexter, and Allison.*)

DEXTER: Great! This is the meeting where we sell Allison to the gypsies, right?

ALLISON: (*laughing*) Very funny, Dexter. We're going to sell you to the circus.

MR. COLEMAN: No, we're not. He's too good a basketball player. We're going to trade him to the Boston Celtics for Larry Bird.

ALLISON: What kind of bird is that?
(*All laugh.*)

MRS. COLEMAN: I guess we better call this meeting to order before I lose my whole family. Dexter, I believe you're the chairperson tonight.

DEXTER: Okay. The council is now called to order. Who'd like to order first?
(*Allison giggles, but a sharp glance from his parents reminds Dexter to stay on track.*)

DEXTER: I mean, who has a compliment to share?

MR. COLEMAN: Well, I'd like to compliment you on your computer project, Dexter. That computer camp you went to last summer has really paid off. It was an outstanding project.

DEXTER: Thanks. I want to thank Allison for staying out of my room again this week.

ALLISON: And I want to compliment Dexter for teaching me how to play Astron on the computer.

MRS. COLEMAN: And I'd like to compliment both of you for the wonderful dinner you guys made Wednesday.

MR. COLEMAN: Mmmm, yeah. Pizza Surprise! Delicioso!

DEXTER: Are there any more compliments? No? Then let's read the minutes from the last meeting. Dad? You're secretary.

MR. COLEMAN: Let's see. Here we go.
1. Dexter gave the report he promised about our driving to the Grand Canyon next summer.
2. We decided to host all the cousins, aunts, and uncles at our house *next* Thanksgiving.
3. Dexter and Allison agreed to help out by cooking dinner one night each week . . . mmm mmm . . . Pizza Surprise!
(*All laugh as he licks his lips.*)

DEXTER: Is there any old business?
(*Dexter looks at Allison as if by prearrangement.*)

ALLISON: Can we vote about the Grand Canyon now?

MRS. COLEMAN: I can see you guys have been talking. I'm excited about it, too, but remember, we don't vote on things in our family; we discuss them and decide together.

DEXTER: Yeah, we know. Consensus. Well, we ran out of time last week, so let's continue the discussion.

MR. COLEMAN: Sounds good to me, but I did notice a pressing agenda item, so maybe we should agree to limit discussion to fifteen minutes.

DEXTER: (*looks at Allison and grimaces*) Okay, I guess. Does everyone agree to limit discussion on the Grand Canyon to fifteen minutes? Okay, who wants to begin?

MRS. COLEMAN: I checked at work, and the end of July would be good for me.

MR. COLEMAN: Two weeks then would be good for me too, but then I might not be able to get away for the beach like we usually do over the 4th.

DEXTER: We could skip the beach and go swimming in the Colorado River. Allison, would you like to go body surfing in Lava Falls?

MRS. COLEMAN: Very cute, Dexter Coleman. Maybe you could demonstrate how to body surf in the twenty-foot waves of Lava Falls for her.

DEXTER: Just kidding, Mom. But how about the dates?

(*Ten minutes.*)

MR. COLEMAN:	(*reading his notes*) So, we agree to leave home at 5:00 A.M. on the morning of July 17, so that we can make it to the first campground by early afternoon—in time to set up the tents and go swimming. We will car camp—staying at the parks that Dex found in his report—until we reach the canyon. Your mother will call tomorrow to see what kind of trips into the canyon are available and we'll discuss those next week.
DEXTER AND ALLISON:	Yeah!
DEXTER:	Is there any bank business? No? Okay, then, Mom, will you pass out the allowances? (*Mrs. Coleman gives Allison and Dexter their weekly allowances.*)
DEXTER:	Thanks, I needed that!
ALLISON:	Thanks, I needed that, too!
MR. COLEMAN:	How about new business, Dex?
DEXTER:	Oh, okay. It says on the agenda "Dexter hit me (Allison)."
MRS. COLEMAN:	Since this involves you, Dex, would you like me to take over as chairperson for a few minutes?
DEXTER:	Yeah, I guess you better.
MRS. COLEMAN:	Okay, Allison, can you tell the council what happened? [**This is Step 1 of the problem-solving process described on page 138.**]
ALLISON:	Yes. I was watching the TV and Dexter told me that he wanted to watch a football game. I told him, "Not now, Dexter." Then he hit me.
MRS. COLEMAN:	Do you want to add anything, Dex?
DEXTER:	That wasn't exactly the way it happened. I had been waiting all week for this game, and Allison was watching some dumb cartoon.
ALLISON:	It's not dumb!
MRS. COLEMAN:	Allison, it's Dex's turn. Dex, can you tell your side without insulting?
DEXTER:	Okay. Anyway, I told her she could watch it in your room, but that since the game was only on cable, I had to watch in here. So I changed the channel, but she kept changing it back. So I told her if she changed it one more time, I would smack her.

ALLISON: Then he hit me right here on my shoulder.

MRS. COLEMAN: Allison, do you agree that's what happened?

ALLISON: Yes.

MS. COLEMAN: Okay, who would like to share? [**Step 2.**]

MR. COLEMAN: Well, it sounds like Allison was egging Dex on a little. But Dex, you know the family rule is no hitting except in self-defense.

MRS. COLEMAN: Right. That's what bothers me, too.

DEXTER: I know, but she can get me so mad!

ALLISON: Well, it's not just your TV!

DEXTER: I know, but you could have watched your show on the other set.

MR. COLEMAN: Well, Allison?

ALLISON: I guess so.

MRS. COLEMAN: Any more sharing? Then let's hear some suggestions. [**Step 3.**]

DEXTER: I'll apologize for hitting her if she will apologize for hogging the TV.

MR. COLEMAN: Maybe we can all agree that if someone wants to watch a cable show, and the other person has a regular show, the cable person can have the TV in here.

MRS. COLEMAN: That sounds like a good idea. But I think Dex should also pay a consequence for breaking the no-hitting rule.

MR. COLEMAN: What do you suggest?

MRS. COLEMAN: I don't know. Dex, what do you think?

DEXTER: Yeah, okay. I guess I could clean the gutters for Dad.

MR. COLEMAN: I'd love the help, son, but don't you think the consequence should relate to Allison some way?

MRS. COLEMAN: Maybe Dex could give the family a free babysitting—whoops, excuse me, Allison—I mean a free kidsitting. Are there any other ideas? Okay, let's decide. [**Step 4.**]

DEXTER: I don't mind kidsitting. I guess that's more logical.

MRS. COLEMAN: Allison, what do you think?

ALLISON: I want him to promise not to hit me anymore.

DEXTER: Okay, I promise.

MRS. COLEMAN: I'm glad. Now, Allison, what about Dex's kidsitting as a consequence?

ALLISON: Okay.

MRS. COLEMAN: Is everyone agreed? Great, we have consensus. Honey, will you read the agreement?

MR. COLEMAN: We, the Coleman family, agree that . . . Oh, did we get consensus on the new TV agreement?

MRS. COLEMAN: Oh, thanks. Does everyone agree that the cable TV will be used by the person who wants to watch a cable show, and the other person will watch the TV in our room? Fine.

MR. COLEMAN: Okay, the other agreement reads, "Dexter apologizes for hitting Allison and agrees to kidsit one time free as a consequence. He also agrees *never* to hit her again."

MRS. COLEMAN: Anything else on that? Then it looks like it's time for our treat. Allison, it's your turn. Did you make another fruit salad like last month?

ALLISON: Nope.
(She runs to the kitchen and returns with a platter.)

DAD: Just what I wanted. A piece of leftover Pizza Surprise!

11

Raising a "We" Generation

In our children rests the future of the people!

ALFRED ADLER

One of the themes of this book has been that thriving in a democratic society requires cooperation—a sense that we are all in this together. In fact, the theme of cooperation runs through the history of every democratic nation on earth. None of us is as great as all of us, and so by combining resources and talents, we all come out ahead.

The spirit of cooperation, however, has fallen on hard times. I, and perhaps you, belong to a generation that has been branded the "me" generation, a label associated with self-centeredness, narcissism, and a preoccupation with looking out for #1. Personal growth and personal satisfaction have become the goals that have replaced the broader social concerns of earlier eras. The "me" generation, in fact, is clearly a rebellion—a reaction against what might be called the "thee" generation of the 1960s—a generation so full of a sense of purpose and power that it did not know its own limits.

Neither the "thees" nor the "mes" have to win out. Instead, each can contribute to something new—a synthesis of both. The "thee" generation is strong in the knowledge that the world is an interrelated place—that what happens in one part of the world affects everyone, that what happens to the poorest of us concerns all of us. The "me" generation, on the other hand, has learned that freedom always occurs within limits—and that power and intervention also have limits. Its members have also contributed a new sense of self-reliance as they have learned how to stand firmly on their own legs.

What might a synthesis of these generations look like? Perhaps a spirit might develop that we are in this together, and that together each of us can develop self-reliance as well as cooperation with others. Shall we cooperate by joining together to rear a "we" generation? Encouraging an attitude of "we-ness" is similar to encouraging any other attitude or value in your child. You can use the skills you have already learned in this book for this purpose. Only the specifics change. What are our tools? Let's review.

A Review of the Skills You've Learned

Parenting skills can be divided into two general categories: encouragement skills (those that move the child ahead) and discipline skills (those that set limits or stop the child's movement). By using both kinds of skills, you can influence your child toward certain behaviors and values, and away from others. Look at the chart on page 148 to review how these break down. (The page numbers indicate where each skill was first presented.)

Encouraging Values and Attitudes
(Such as "We-ness")

As we have noted, the best way to teach values and attitudes is to emphasize the positive—encourage your child's positive approaches to his or her basic goals. Let's review the elements of encouragement, focusing on how we can best encourage "we-ness."

Avoid discouraging. Learning positive values requires positive self-esteem and courage. Avoiding the discouragement traps is therefore an important beginning. You particularly want to avoid discouraging

ENCOURAGEMENT SKILLS	DISCIPLINE SKILLS
■ Avoid disouraging (61)	■ Assess the purpose of misbehavior (45)
■ Focus on strengths (75)	■ Avoid paying off the mistaken approach (49)
■ Show confidence (73)	
■ Value child as is (78)	■ Send "I" messages (105)
■ Stimulate independence (80)	■ Allow natural consequences (116)
■ Use active communication (124)	■ Use logical consequences (108)
■ Hold family council meetings (133)	■ Use active problem solving in family council meetings (138)
■ Create family enrichment activities (86)	

movement toward the desired value. Avoid focusing your attention on the times your child is selfish or uncooperative.

Focus on strengths. Look for signs of "we-ness"; then acknowledge the effort.

■ "Thanks for pitching in; you were a big help."

■ "Isn't it great how fast it gets done when we all work together?"

■ "I sure liked the way you included your brother in the conversation."

If your child is fairly young, use bedtime as a time to focus on particular values. These two questions might help stimulate "we-ness" (as well as self-esteem):

■ "What did you learn today?"

■ "How did you help somebody today."

Show confidence. Help your child understand that he or she is capable and has much to contribute.

■ "You can do it."

■ "I think you can."

■ "You can be a big help by _____."

■ "Don't give up. I know you'll get it if you stick with it."

Value your child as he or she is. Let your child know that he or she is special, unique, one of a kind, one in four billion! At the same time, let this special child know that he or she also is part of the group— the family, the school, the city, state, country, race, religion, and even planet. Express pride in each group that you belong to, and teach respect for other people's groups as well (because ultimately we are all in at least one group with everyone else: humanity).

- "You're a Greenhaw, Margie. Don't forget that."
- "How do you think that our family is like families in Russia?"

Stimulate independence (and interdependence). As the "me" generation has rekindled a desire for independence and the "thee" generation focused on our mutual dependence on each other, a "we" generation will know that we are all interdependent. In other words, the world best thrives through strong individuals and strong nations that have the courage to depend on each other as well as themselves.

- "I bet you can do that by yourself now."
- "What if I hold the ladder while you paint?"
- "Nice job, Michelangelo!"

Use active communication. This is a "we" process for helping your child solve problems. The experience of having the support and guidance of another when he or she is faced with a problem helps to reaffirm that we do need one another. Take time to use active communication skills with your child regularly.

- "Hey. You look really down. What's the story?"

Hold family council meetings. This is the epitome of "we-ness." Family council meetings teach children how to work as a team, and they can foster a tremendous sense of belonging. However, they are highly structured, time-consuming events that many families do not have the discipline to continue regularly. My hope is that you will work at it until it is no longer an effort. When family council meetings become a natural part of your family, you will be very glad that you stuck with this process.

To help undercut sibling rivalry and foster a sense of "we-ness," plan family celebrations in which all participate in a family member's success on a special occasion. In other words, when anyone in the family succeeds, everyone gets to enjoy the celebration—whether it's a special meal, a cake, or an event.

Create family enrichment activities. Each of the enrichment activities suggested in the book helps foster a sense of "we-ness." Particularly, the concept of mutual respect can help your child learn that not only is he or she important, but so is the other person.

- "I don't call you names. Please don't call me names."

- "I don't hit you. Please don't hit me."

Disciplining Misbehavior to Teach Values and Attitudes (Such as "We-ness")

While the best method of teaching values is through a combination of encouragement and positive modeling (that is, setting a good example), discipline can also be helpful. Discipline can set limits and thereby teach children what not to do.

To teach "we-ness," we want to limit selfishness, failures to pitch in or otherwise contribute to the group, and lack of concern or respect for others. Two notes of caution, however, are in order:

1. Do not interpret the normal need to be alone from time to time (the basic goal of withdrawal) and a desire for independence (the basic goal of power) as a problem. We should encourage, rather than limit, such behavior, recognizing that a certain degree of "me-ness" is an essential part of "we-ness."

2. Keep in mind that punishment is not a useful form of discipline. If we hurt the child for behaving selfishly, the child may become more discouraged and launch a power struggle or revenge cycle. Neither response will foster cooperation.

Assess the purpose of misbehavior. Remember, we always want to assess the child's mistaken purpose before we take a corrective action. Otherwise, we may continue to pay off the child's approach, thereby helping to keep the misbehavior going. Refer to the chart on page 54 to refresh your memory about how to differentiate among seeking undue attention, rebellion, seeking revenge, and avoidance.

Avoid paying off the mistaken approach. Use this chart to refresh your memory about what *not* to do when your child misbehaves.

IF THE APPROACH IS	AVOID
Seeking undue attention	Nagging, coaxing, reminding, and so on
Rebellion	Fighting or giving in
Seeking revenge	Hurting back
Avoidance	Giving up

NOTE: Children often pursue their own needs and wants as they begin to feel their own power. The phrase "I want what I want when I want it" typifies the attitude of most children at one time or another. When they begin learning that the world does not work that way (except at some Grandmas' houses), they often rebel, and a power struggle ensues. This often happens during the second year of life, hence the label "terrible twos." Because children often fail to leave this "me—I want" attitude in their twos, power struggles often occur throughout childhood. As you teach the value of "we-ness," be especially on guard to sidestep these power struggles. In other words, don't fight *and* don't give in.

Send "I" messages. Good, clear, nonblaming communication is often enough to set limits. "I" messages not only establish limits, but they also let children know what *is* wanted of them. Then your encouragement skills can build on this beginning.

- "When you don't do your job, I feel let down, because the whole house doesn't run as well. I'd like you to complete the vacuuming before dinner."

- "When you go to the refrigerator to get a snack and don't ask us if we would like something, I feel a little taken advantage of because of all the times I bring you something. I'd appreciate it if you would think to offer me a snack, too."

Allow natural consequences. One of the natural consequences of being too self-centered is that the child often loses friends. Helping your child make the connection between such behavior and this consequence is a sensitive job and requires your best active communication skills.

Use logical consequences. When "I" messages are not successful and natural consequences are not available, employing logical consequences is the discipline of choice. Specifically, you can use either when-then or either-or choices to help limit certain values by limiting the behaviors that express those values. For example:

VALUE TO LIMIT	EXPRESSIVE BEHAVIOR	CHOICE OF LOGICAL CONSEQUENCES
Being selfish	Not taking turns	"When you are ready for me to have a turn, let me know, and we can continue playing" [parent leaves].
Not helping	Failure to do a chore	"When you have finished vacuuming [your job], then I will cook dinner [my job]."
Showing disrespect	Name calling	"Either talk to me without calling me names or the discussion ends right now. You decide."

Use active problem solving in family council meetings. Remembering the wisdom of George Washington that people are more apt to abide by rules that they have had input in making, active problem solving can be very useful in teaching "we-ness." Some items that you might put on your family agenda to decide upon through active problem solving:

- Planning the family vacation.

- Planning a week's menu.

- Assessing how family members help each other.

- Discussing specific situations where one family member wanted support from another family member, but did not get it.

- Resolving any problem between family members.

The Most Important Family in the World

The final step in both strengthening your own family and helping to raise a "we" generation is to emphasize the family unit. Whether you belong to a traditional nuclear family, a one-parent family, or a step-family, I feel that this family unit is so important that it deserves special emphasis, not just today, but throughout the century, and not just in your family, but throughout the human community.

Families have been the backbone of civilization since human beings discovered that we could not only survive but also thrive by forming small, cooperative units. Families have also been a source of support, encouragement, and sustenance. They have pulled us through time and time again against overwhelming odds.

Let your children know that they are part of a family. Plan frequent family activities; use phrases like "in our family . . ."; and develop your own family traditions and rituals. Your family is the most important family in the world to your children. And through your family, your children will come to learn that they belong to the much larger family of humanity. Their contributions will determine the shape of that family tomorrow, for "in our children rests the future of the people!"

Appendix

Tips for Encouraging a Resistant Spouse to Read This Book

If you found this book helpful and think that your spouse would appreciate the Active Parenting approach, then it's a simple matter of making a friendly recommendation. But spouses often resist a new approach. These tips assume that you either anticipate resistance or that your spouse has already declined to read this book.

1. Avoid coming across as if you have just come down from Mt. Sinai with the Ten Commandments. A better approach might be, "Some of this sounds pretty good; other parts I'm not sure about. I wonder what you think?"

2. Avoid criticizing your spouse's way of being a parent. Especially avoid beginning sentences with, "The book says . . ." And under no circumstances begin a sentence with the awful words, "Dr. Popkin says . . ."

3. Be subtle. Leave a copy of the book in a place where your spouse might pick it up.

4. Use your encouragement skills. If your partner chances to begin reading, be interested in his or her opinion. Find areas of agreement (not disagreement), and avoid putting him or her down.

5. Try recommending specific passages that you think your partner will like as a method of gaining his or her interest.

6. Most of all, concentrate on improving your own relationship with your children. Your partner may learn some of these skills through

your example (modeling). He or she may even begin asking you questions. If this good fortune occurs, you will want to resist the temptation to say, "If you had read the damn book as I'd asked, you'd *know* why I did that!" Instead, encourage this interest by talking about the skill or principle, and then gently offering your spouse a chance to read more.

Related Reading

Albert, Linda. *Coping with Kids.* New York: E. P. Dutton, 1984.

Curran, Dolores. *Traits of a Healthy Family.* Minneapolis: Winston Press, 1983.

Davitz, Lois, and Joel Davitz. *How to Live (Almost Happily) with a Teenager.* Minneapolis: Winston Press, 1982.

Dinkmeyer, Don, and Gary D. McKay. *Raising a Responsible Child: Practical Steps to Successful Family Relationships.* New York: Simon and Schuster, 1973.

Dreikurs, Rudolf, and Vicki Soltz. *Children: The Challenge.* New York: E. P. Dutton, 1964.

Ellis, Albert. *A Guide to Rational Living.* Englewood Cliffs, NJ: Prentice-Hall, 1961.

Ginott, Haim G. *Between Parent and Child.* New York: Macmillan, 1965.

Gordon, Thomas. *Parent Effectiveness Training.* New York: Peter H. Wyden, 1971.

Lillard, P. P. *Montessori: A Modern Approach.* New York: Schocken Books, 1972.

Index

People to Lead an Exciting New Video-Based Parenting Program

What is "Active Parenting: A Video-Based Program"?

Active Parenting is a six-session program that uses a combination of learning methods to more effectively teach the skills presented in this book. Built around forty-five brief video scenes portrayed by three "families" (played expertly by professional actors), Active Parenting also includes group activities, readings, and home practice activities. A typical Active Parenting group includes a leader and fifteen to twenty parents who meet one evening a week for six weeks (about two hours a session).

Who Can Lead an Active Parenting Group?

Most Active Parenting leaders are helping professionals such as counselors, teachers, social workers, psychologists, ministers, nurses, and others. Some are concerned parents who enjoy leading group discussions and facilitating the activities that make Active Parenting the most advanced parent education program available anywhere. Some leaders prepare for leading their groups by participating in one of our optional one-day Active Parenting leader certification workshops. Others prefer to rely on the detailed Leader's Guide and their own experience.

What Does the Program Offer That This Book Doesn't?

Visual reinforcement. You have already met our three video families, the Colemans, the Bradfords, and the Clarkes, in the case studies presented in this book. The videotapes make them come alive as they deal with many more of the typical family problems that we have been discussing. Video can help you better retain the skills that you have learned in this book. Our language is filled with phrases (like "seeing is believing") that highlight one fact: the majority of us are visual learners. You will find that an Active Parenting group will help you remember what to do at that moment when you need it the most—namely, when *your* child is testing his or her limits.

Parents supporting parents. More and more parents are recognizing their need for skills, support, and information. When ten to twenty such parents gather together in an Active Parenting group with a concerned leader, something extraordinary happens. A sense of cohesiveness and mutual support develops. Parents come to understand that they are not alone with their doubts and difficulties in being parents. And best of all, they help each other learn, so that problems get solved and families grow stronger.

How Can You Get a Group Going in Your Community?

Most Active Parenting groups are sponsored by either a school, church or synagogue, mental health center, or private professional. If you want to make Active Parenting happen in your community, the first step is to contact someone in one of these organizations and explain what you want. Ask that person to write us for an information packet that explains the program in detail (or write us yourself). Then offer your support in helping to get the first Active Parenting group off the ground (experience shows that parents spread the word on their own after the first group).

For Further Information Contact:
ACTIVE PARENTING
4669 Roswell Road NE
Atlanta, GA 30342

As of this printing, there are more than two thousand Active Parenting groups in the U.S. alone. We hope that your community will join us.